Rūḥ al-Quds

Hermetic Illuminations

A Holy Mother Sourcebook

by
Lee Irwin

Raa-Nub

Hermetic Illuminations
A Holy Mother Sourcebook

Cover and Book Design by Jeremy Berg

Published by Lorian Press LLC

ISBN: 978-1-939790-78-1

Irwin, Lee
Hermetic Illuminations: A Holy Mother Sourcebook/Lee Irwin

First Edition: May 2025

Printed in the United States of America,
United Kingdon and Australia

www.lorian.org

Table of Contents

Part Two

Part Three

Introduction
By David Spangler

For sixty years, my work has been to translate wisdom, insights, impressions, intuitions, and communications from a higher, non-physical reality into concepts and language that are accessible to my readers and students. This work has been both an assignment—a job my soul has taken on—and a joy.

It has also been a challenge, a frustrating one at times.

The reason is not hard to understand. Once one steps in consciousness and attunement beyond the familiar territory of incarnate life, one discovers oneself in touch with a multi-layered, multi-dimensional world filled with paradox and modes of being that transcend the bounds of time and space as we regularly conceive of and experience them. The contours of this subtle and spiritual reality rarely coincide with those of our physical world.

How to convey this?

How does one describe the color blue to someone who has been blind since birth? How to describe the flavor of an orange to someone who has never seen or heard of this fruit?

How to convey the reality of a living cosmos filled from top to bottom, from the infinitely large to the infinitely small, with sentiency and awareness? How to convey the love, the joy, the creative exuberance that is an integral part of this cosmos?

How to convey our oneness with this living universe and at the same time, the value and importance of our individual life within it, without one eclipsing or diminishing the other?

This has been the challenge of mystics and contemplatives throughout history.

I have often used metaphor as a way of describing the otherwise indescribable. Because of my science background, I draw on ecology and physics for these metaphors. To say that the subtle worlds are the Earth's "second ecology," with spiritual beings such as angels being a "noetic species," helps to convey, I hope, the interconnectedness and interdependency of life in the subtle realms—much like an ecosystem in the physical world—and that the beings who inhabit this subtle ecology are natural, not supernatural. They belong to a Nature that transcends in many ways the conditions we customarily use to define what is "natural." They are, in their domain, "ordinary," albeit a sacred ordinariness that at this moment in our own evolution can seem extraordinary.

Metaphor, though, has its limits. It requires attention and discernment to go beyond the image to the larger reality which it imperfectly represents. Are the subtle and spiritual realms truly an ecology? In one sense, yes, but the interconnectedness and interpenetration of beings one with another in expanding domains of consciousness and love goes far beyond anything a physical ecology can manifest.

In other words, one can't take metaphors literally.

Yet, one can't dismiss them as mere poetry, either. They can be needed and important bridges across the chasm of the unknown; we just can't make them the destination.

This requires *discernment*, an ability to perceive ever deeper levels of reality. This is a function of the heart as much as of the mind, and of the soulful heart, at that.

One of my spiritual mentors and colleagues first appeared to me in the form of a college professor, a middle-aged man wearing a tweed jacket with leather elbow patches. At the time, this was a concrete vision I could understand and to which I could relate, having just left the university environment myself. But I knew at the same time that this being, whom I called "John," was more than what I was psychically seeing. There was a Light, a Presence, within him that was far more real and vital than the image of the college professor. In a way, the latter was itself a metaphor, projected by his consciousness to my imagination as a way of making contact. Later, he dropped this appearance, and I had to learn how to follow him inward, so to speak, beyond form and into the heart-presence and Light of his own sacred nature.

We all have this sacred nature within us; indeed, everything in the world from the tiniest atom to the most distant galaxy does. Accepting this and striving to be aware of this shared Presence of Light is a vital step in learning to commune and communicate with the subtle and spiritual worlds. It is the Light of our kinship with the rest of creation and the secret language by means of which all things are known to each other.

We know this Presence through our ability to embody it, which is above all else, an act of love: love of self, love of world, love of the Whole that is within and behind all things. It is, I have discovered, not through psychic or mystical perceptions that one bridges the chasm between earthly and spiritual realities but through love and through embodiment. The discipline and practice of communication with subtle and spiritual realms is at heart a discipline and practice of embodiment.

Which brings me to this book.

Lee is one of the most discerning people I know. When it comes to navigating the sacred terrain that is around and within us, he knows whereof he writes through his own practice and experience. He sees beyond the forms, both literal and metaphorical, that are instruments but not the wholeness of Spirit.

But more than that, he *is* that of which he writes.

Lee writes:

The greatest book of Wisdom is the well-lived, compassionate, exemplary life; no text is greater than the living soul embodied, holding the dignity, grace, joy, and abundance of Spirit that results in teachings worthy of memory. We remember how compassionate, forgiving, loving, joyful, humble, kind, thoughtful, responsible, exemplary were those we learned from, who taught us in the living flesh, how better to be human and embrace our sacredness. (10.10)

The greatest book is the Book of Life, the unwritten text of our desire and struggle to perfect our understanding, love, care, and concern for the world and all its creatures. The greatest teaching is by example; the greatest gift, the giving of our attention to what matters, knowing how to discard personal distractions for the embodiment of our beloved Ideals. (10.11)

In this book, you hold in your hands a treasure, wisdom distilled from a lifetime of spiritual study, reflection, attunement, and practice. The reason is that Lee embodies the "Holy Mother Spirit" of which he writes. When someone embodies this Presence, his or her words become translucent to the higher realities.

I have had the pleasure of knowing Lee for over thirty years. He embodies the scholar, the teacher, the mystic, the psychic, and the contemplative. For many years, he headed up his own construction crew, so he is also a man who can build a house, a carpenter, a plumber, an electrician. He is a man of practical earthly skills as well as of transcendental skills.

He is a man who embodies and practices the loving heart open to the wonders of a sentient, living universe. It is why he can write confidently and poetically about this greater Reality that embraces us all.

And because of this, his words resonate with an authenticity and attunement that transcends language and metaphor and offers the attentive and soulful reader engagement with the Light at the heart of all.

This book is a contemplative companion, a work to come back to again and again, not for its words alone but for the unfolding and ever-emerging spirit that it represents, with each reading offering new discovery and delight.

Thank you, Lee, for a lifetime's wisdom offered in these pages.

David Spangler
January 2025

Foreword

The challenge of reading this work is to allow the full scope of its inspiration to speak poetically and aesthetically, in analogical signs, as a testimony of soulful knowing. An additional challenge is to avoid the tendency to translate what is written into ideas informed by beliefs other than those of the author. Reading is an art, one easily lost in the surface languages of popular culture and electronic media, in the impulses for immediate comprehension, as though words were a sufficient medium for understanding. But words are only a shadow cast by a light illumining heart and mind seeking to express what lies beyond surface appearance, beyond what is written. A word is a form, one with multiple ramifications and multiple meanings, a bird whose flight cannot be predicted by its color or shape. Tracking the flight of these words leads to an open sky, a dawning twilight of diverse shades of meaning, any phrase or term can lead to new thoughts and subtle insights.

The mind of the reader must be prepared for a journey, one whose goal is to prompt the soul for an awakening to Spirit through Mystery, through illumination guided by a deep desire to experience a heart-felt encounter with the deep source of Being, the source of all words and thoughts. It is a book of prayers, songs, poems and heart-felt illuminations directed toward an invisible Presence whose afterglow casts a soft light around each phrase when read with a similar ardor and desire for insight and inspiration. The author has spent decades composing this work, not by rewriting or changing what was written but because the verses and themes came only slowly over many years of receptivity to what was emerging. Slowly each section was composed and then allowed to sit unchanged, sometimes for years, until another section was inspired. Like a tree growing in a garden of mystical delights, this book grew its roots into the sacred soil of Being and its branches into the open sky of cosmos and the astral heavens. The three parts of the book refer to three phases of the author's life, from late midlife (40s), to older life (60s), to elderhood (now 80), each with its own emphasis and concerns.

The reference to Hermetic Illuminations sets the tone for the alchemical nature of what is communicated, not a technique or praxis, but a stance that is reverent with regards to the eternal beauty and luster of all feminine-masculine Godliness. The Hermetic tradition teaches spiritual illumination through gnosis as an open process of discovery guided by intuitions, received as spontaneous awakening to that deeper ground or what I call the Holy Mother, the Beloved Presence. Sophia, as Divine Feminine image, is a primary Hermetic Archon who hovers over this work, an august figure of great purity and kindness, transmitting a sacred task, the transcription of spiritual truths into a narrative of hope, beauty, and peace. Love is at the heart of this work, a love received and transmitted in accord with an unseen Mystery, a Hermetic Illumination of soul gained over a lifetime of seeking. It is a work meant for the few and the many, a poetic affirmation pointing beyond itself to a higher reality than words can express.

To receive such inspiration is a gift, a grace, an offering made at the altar of the ever-enduring Now in which there is no surplus, only a sufficient approximation of Infinite possibility made explicit and visual. There is so much more that cannot be held by the words but only known by the illumined heart, such that the text is only a shadow of that greater Ultimacy before which all words become exhausted and end as glistening shells on a beach whose shore is no more than an island surrounded by the unfathomable depth and flow of Ocean. Some words become a raft, a craft meant to carry the reader to a new level of perception, to new insights, new possible outcomes, applicable only through assimilation and transformation. The goal is not the inculcation of a teaching, but an awakening to insight which frees the reader from all texts, traditions, rafts, and words—free to discover a nuance, a shared contribution to our collective All-Becoming.

Let us read with respect, not with pride or notions of our self-importance, respect not for the author, but for the Source, however hidden it may be in the turbulence of words and ideas. What lies hidden here is meant to sparkle, gem-like, a golden talisman, indicating a touchstone, where the mind, the word, and the heart fused into a moment of profound synthesis. The almond has a shell, and this represents the words as they stand alone, but in the shell, there is an almond, the sweet taste acquired when the shell is broken open. But even more the almond can be squeezed to produce a sweet oil, and that oil, neither east nor west, is sufficient to light the lamp of the heart in order to create the glow of Living Presence. That is the gift to be desired, not the words, not the ideas, not the thought or intuition, but the actual Presence transmitted to the readers soulful awareness.

Read with compassion and love to discover a Mystery—the Mystery of our immediate, shared spiritual awakening. Have humility and realize that this awakening happens only slowly and takes many years of preparation; do not be impatient, time will pass, the illusions fade, and what endures will be an undying Now replete with a vast horizon far beyond all words and ideas. Have the courage to see your limitations, then seek to overcome them modestly, with grace, and without pretensions. With inner stillness, time will vanish and a greater Now will be born in which all words spoken will become sacred texts, greater than what is written here but harmoniously similar. Such is the goal, to use words as a basis for soul flight beyond the boundaries of everyday thought and into an Infinite Now, into Hermetic Illuminations.

With great appreciation,

Lee Irwin / Sirr al-Basir

البَصِيرُ جَلَّجَلَالُهُ

Opening Prayer
Holy Mother Spirit

There is no light but Thy Light,
No wind without Thy breath
No wave without Thy water
No warmth without Thy fire
No earth without Thy foundation.

No measurable depths without
the joy of Thy Immeasurability
No great heights without
the boundary of Thy Boundlessness
No strong contractions without
the luster of Thy Release
No expansive clarity without
the luminosity of Thy Love.

Oh Blessed Mother Holy Spirit, Spirit Holy Mother,
Holy, Holy, Spirit Mother, Mother Spirit Holy

Hear our prayers, our thoughts, our desires
to Hold and be Held
in Thy bright flame that burns away all dross,
all loss, all sorrow, pain, and suffering
purifying through Thy Grace.

In the cool and healing water, to sense
Thy life-giving fragrance
Thy Flower, the golden lovely lotus
of Thy healing springs,
in the bright hours that Dawning brings.

Oh Blessed Mother Spirit, Holy Spirit Mother
Spirit, Spirit, Holy Mother Spirit, Spirit Holy Mother
O Mother, Hear our Prayers!

A Declaration (1)

This book, spirit-born of flesh and fire, holds the pattern of a realization whose Mystery cannot be inscribed with ink or water or blood. It cannot, before many words are written, be written in any form, nor translated into comprehensible signs, simply to make it clear. It is a work of the heart, of soul, of spirit's grace, of sorrows and joys and dreams, a calling and a declaration. It is a sign, a sacred work whose scope and voice offer a gift, a marker in the fabric of time that divides before and after. (1:1)

What is born of flesh cannot endure beyond death but what is born of spirit and soul endures long, longer than what flesh conceives, endures and thrives and becomes a vessel of the energies of true creation. The holarchy of love's degrees are not held within the concretions of mind, nor thought, nor imagination but only in the vastness of love's overflowing embrace can we know, beyond all doubts, the dignity of our deepest soul desire. (1:2)

We stand on a precipice, balanced on a cliff edge, walk across the void of our doubts on swaying bridges built by the ropes of reason, hope, belief, and handed down traditions. Such fragile bridges! Though we make them of hardened metal, they cannot endure as flesh cannot endure, for where spirit moves freely, our thoughts are leaden, our bodies lag, our faith collapses, and our ideals become only distant images in a darkening sky. (1:3)

There is a wound in the heart of many, a wound caused by war, loss, grief, poverty, suffering, inequality, and indifference toward life agitated by pride, arrogance, distain, and the having of too much or too little. The souls of many are constricted, caught in the increasing contrasts between a soul's desire for dawning light and the darkening shadows of ignorance, fear, anxiety, and dread. The source of that dread is the soul's denial, a vanquishing of spirit, a loss of center. (1:4)

Many are those who believe in soul and many are those who disbelieve. Thus, spirit lags in the minds of many, contested, reduced to paradigms and metaphors of human thought, not loved, or felt deep down in the recesses of our inmost creative being. Rather, held in static images hampered by sorrowing thoughts, fantasized in immature images, rationalized or traditionalized, soul becomes a commodity in the marketplace of spiritual transformation, bought and sold. (1:5)

You are soul, a living presence come again to endure the challenges of flesh for the benefits of all; or you are nothing more than mind and flesh, where feelings come and go. Or you are a morass of conflicting intuitions, drawn this way and that for no good reason other than your momentary pleasures or needs or responsibilities. Or you live submerged, not quite knowing but wanting wisdom without the discipline of learning; you crave but find no satiation. (1:6)

Or you are too learned, too inflated with knowing, too sure of the certainties of sense and reason, too filled with burdens of proof, too heavy with justice or retribution, too weighed down with care and requirements, too circumspect, too detached, too caught in the web of intrigue, too indulgent, too dependent, too self-denying, too bold, too blind. Thus deaf, hobbled, wrapped in layers of material thought, there is no soul, no freedom, no real tomorrow. (1:7)

But soul is there, true and lasting, born from afar and standing near, your very breath, your very being, not the painted images, but the reality of you. Soul is a deep fullness whose immeasurable depths cannot be plumbed by thought or feeling or intuition. Our body is held in a Mystery whose expansive field has no formal boundary, an identity resonant across a cosmos of possible being-in and being-with, an immediacy of Now without limits, a vastness irreducible to a single point of view. (1:8)

We see the boundary and say it cannot be passed, then we

pass it. We bind our self with thought and belief, then say we understand the distinction between truth and illusion. But such knowing is not a deep knowing, it floats on a surface of communal convention, collective habit, and the under-currents of transmitted presupposition or barricades itself behind an esoteric mastery, in science, in art, in spirituality. All boundaries are passable, all illusions transparent. (1:9)

My soul called me and I heard its cry. My soul longed and I felt it's longing. My soul desired and I followed the scent of its heat and the coolness of its spent passion. My soul was willing and I willed that it be so; it longed and I loved; it lost and I gained wisdom; it fell and gave me the strength to go on; it gifted me with the sorrows of others, I was weakened but my soul grew stronger. It was a song of songs, I learned its melody, heard its rhythm, and acknowledged its call. (1:10)

If a bird rests in a tree, surely other birds will rest there as well; thus, my soul sought comfort with soulful others and our songs blended, and many were those whose comfort guided me. For the soul of my soul was lightened by the soul of another, lifted by a soul-shared love, expanded through the shared ardor of our seeking; how many are the souls that guided me! The Eros of our soul's contact was a making of more soul, a harmony of three—self, other, and Mystery. (1:11)

Soul was not lost but found through relatedness, through mergence, through harmonic energies of give and take, through the mysteries of love and the sorrows of separation. There is a communion of souls, an intersection of multiple powers of human possibility that lifts us beyond the merits of our individual capacities. This shared unity of soulfulness is a great blessing and a challenge to yet remain a truthful self, to embody a soulful, deeply felt life, to continue forth even in loss and separation. (1:12)

Not by Soul Alone (2)

It is not by soul alone that the knowing comes, though soul is the medium, the Source is deeper yet, beyond senses, feelings, thoughts, and imaginings. Without soul, we are wrapped in mind's materiality, swathed in gauzy layers, captivated by sensory impression and reasonable or unreasonable thoughts and feelings. With soul, we unravel the boundary and open to a new immensity no longer defined by body, but body held, like the wick of a candle that births a flame. (2:1)

Soul is a field, an energy of conscious being, an index of awareness held within flesh and form, intermediary, a self-expressed continuity of identity bound by patterns of reflected aspiration and desire. Soul opens by degrees to the possibilities of That Which Is and as a ground of contraction to That Which Is Not — neither is true, both dissolve into a vanishing of opposites in order to give birth to a deeper soulfulness, a Third, a *tertium quid*, not captured by either limits or limitlessness. (2:2)

Before soul, before mind, before heart and sense, before feeling and desire, there is a longing and this longing, like the cry of eagle to her young, is an energy of co-creation that gives birth to multiplicity, difference, and uniqueness. The soul does not create alone, it does not live, exist, abide, without its Other, does not thrive without the harmonies of multiple voices, without many dreams, visions, or aesthetic intuitions. Soul alone is not soul. (2:3)

Without the impact of the world, its beauty, mystery, and holy Otherness, without an Eros of Relation, soul cannot expand into the medium of its spiritual capacities. This Otherness is a multitude, not a singularity; a diversity so great that it seems simple, so vast that it seems one-dimensional, so near, that it seems remote and unknowable. There is no barrier or opposition other than what we co-create, no division except where we choose to divide, no loss but what we give up. (2:4)

Beyond the simple duality of Otherness, beyond its shadowed borders of conflicting wants and needs, where soul lies suspended in sleep, dreaming alternate worlds, there is Light, a dawning energy of awakening. This Light, immeasurable in its depths, ignites a soul spark, kindles the longing, creates an ache for seeing that only Seeing satisfies. It is a Seeing that is also a Knowing, *gnosis*, soul-knowledge, not only of itself but also, of its Source. (2:5)

This Light is filled with color, shades, shadows, depths, diverse and subtle, expansive in nature, invisible to the physical eye, but radiant in the soul's perception, giving form and hue and contour to a multitude of spirit-beings, soulful seekers, to invisible life not bound by cosmic space-time. We all exist in that shared Light, without exception, all are filled with the life-force that it gives, without which we would be not souls, nor bodies, nor minds. (2:6)

It is not only Light, but energy, spirit, love, consciousness, being, bliss and more, an ecstasy of subtle currents flowing through all creation. I called it Holy Mother Spirit, blesséd Source of primordial love and joy, wisdom Mother, source of insight, Spirit Holy Mother bright, an ever-lighting lamp, purest oil of the purest olive, sweetest honey, luminous aura of the Tree of Life, fertile ground for every root, blessed Fruit of every bush and plant and flower. (2:7)

No name can adequately hold that sacred energy, source of life; all words spoken or written or dreamed or heard in visions cannot hold that blesséd Spirit Light. Words can only point, indicate a perception, represent an encounter, echo a felt soulfulness of touch, or taste, of sound like music on a crashing shore in waves, storms, and brightest lightning. Thought cannot hold it, belief cannot reach it, wisdom cannot be it. What Is, surpasses all. (2:8)

Spirit Holy Mother is ever the source of my soul's calling, a longing of soul for wisdom or light or love's touch. She called me and I heard Her song, felt Her touch, I descended into depths where I was lost, where I wandered in a maze of my own making, where I was a child without a guide, a soul immersed who slowly learned to breath more deeply, to increase my depth without gasping, to be a centered Infinite without seeking. (2:9)

Spirit was my Other, then became embodied in the All of

Other's that I loved. She came through the smiles and tears, the joys and sorrows of relationships, through the sunlight on a winter's morning, through the wind and rain, through a blade of grass, a mustard seed, a fire rose, or a sparkling jewel reflected in the eye of my Beloved. There is no fear that cannot be overcome with courage; unity is not without trial, blessedness will test you. (2:10)

Soul is the medium of this encounter; soul, as the matrix of longing and insight, of desire and its satisfactions, must be shaped into a vessel that can hold the intensity of this Love that can then unfold, fill the heart, illumine the mind, purify the etheric layers, elucidate within a harmony of correspondences, a resonant, vibrant clarity of deep knowing. The noetic and psychic aspects must be stable and fully harmonized for such a dawning. (2:11)

Inspiration and guidance are abundant within the matrix of passion's call for soul; one must listen to the Voices of the wind and wave, feel the energies of warmth within the coldest day or darkest night, taste the sweetness within bitter words or anger, feel compassion in isolation and peace in times of trial and decrease. There is no going forward without some degree of falling back, no staying on the path, without missteps, no progress without loss and surrender. (2:12)

The Book of Life (3)

In the Book of Life is written the story of the Holy Mother Spirit, not from one tradition or one culture, but from all peoples, all traditions, all cultures, all worlds. Everywhere there is life and growth, everywhere there is a nurturing presence, a sign of kindness or generosity, there is Spirit Holy Mother. Where there is life, there is Spirit Holy Mother, where there is conscious being, Holy Mother Spirit abides. (3:1)

What is the Book of Life? It is a Book no hand can hold and no tongues pronounce, a Book filled with energies that have no names and processes whose interactions cannot be numbered or described. It is a Book of the chosen and the despised, the loved and hated, the halt and swift, the illumined and ignorant, the quark and cosmos. It is a Book accessible only by a lucid mind liberated from its bondages of doubt and denial, filled with Spirit's grace. (3:2)

The Book of Life is not a record of the saved or elect, not an accounting of deeds of goodness or correct beliefs. It is a Testimony and record of all those who rejoice in Spirit and whose deeds are resonant with life, health, compassion, and a reverent Celebration of the gifts given to every creature, great or small. All life is inscribed in this Book, all the variable forms of being, all the diversities of incarnate perception and response within the webs of life. (3:3)

The unifying Spirit of this holy Book is the energy of love expanded and encompassing without closure or grasping, the complexity and diversity of all spiritual ecologies. Each ecology supports life, gives a context for development, provides a basis for relationships within a field of meaning that unfolds a visionary potential, a creative imagining of the possible. These are the webs of life and the Book is the record of the luminous points within each web. (3:4)

Some luminous points are an intersection between webs, across multiple ecologies, aesthetically connected, spiritually joined, energetically alive, vibrant with life-force, a nexus of Holy Mother Spirit filling the delicate strands of connection with joyful love, insight, and acceptance. The diverse patterns of cocreated life, refracted through these precious drops, assemble and reassemble through etheric process images, our emergent life and many rebirths. (3:5)

There are images within images, refractions within refractions, a jewel net of interdependent relations, like words on a page whose sense can only mean according to the soul and heart of the reader. Such images are a shimmering sign whose symbolism records an emergent subtle order, enigmatic, drawn in by a flaming finger on the palace wall, whose golden letters reflects a wisdom of a higher order, a Holy Spiritual of insight and meaning. (3:6)

The Book of Life is written in the heart of each person, animated by soul-threads of vital life, amplified by deeds, contracted by misdeeds, energized by Presence in a multitude of forms whose meanings cannot be compressed into letters, sounds, or signs. The meaning endures, carried from life to life, from relation to relation, from earth to heaven and back again. A song is sung on every page, without notes or words, music for soul's delight, mixed with longing. (3:7)

I read the Book of Life, felt my heart expand, observed immodesty and fear, desire and hope, love and passion, wonder and terror. I was immobilized, frozen, ecstatic, then slowly thawed, softened, made receptive, taught that within that Light, all is melded, melted into a merging whole, flowing into the deeps of an immense Work whose contours cannot be held by a single world, a single teaching, a single cosmos, a single man, woman, or child. (3:8)

Blesséd are the Words of that Book, how many they are! I heard the Hieros Logoi sound, deep within, like soft echoes on a swelling sea; I saw them through the opaque waters of my own incomprehension. I felt the meanings deepen, releasing me from pain and sorrow, healing old wounds, opening through visionary dreams, an inscrutable content whose syllables were holy chants, prayers, mantra sounds of rhythmic restoration, images beyond counting. (3:9)

The Book of Life is what we live, what we do, say, think, believe, promise, doubt, fear, and confess to others or to our Holy Spirituals, what is seen and known, both near and far. The rhythm of the heart is its solar pulse; the transit of the soul is its lunar beauty inscribed in night dreams sent and received; these energies combine with a multitude of Others, to create through lasting impression, a more wholesome life, a union of Sun and Moon and many Stars. (3:10)

The great Continuum of this Book is the multiple union of worlds, the world awakening to subtle realms not yet seen or known, forthcoming in the Time to Be and the Time that Is. There is a vast communion in this Book, a story of multiple lives, multiple worlds, whole clusters of solar civilizations engaged in a Great Work—the awakening of souls, the transformation of multiple species, the engendering of life, precious, rare, loveliness unspeakable. (3:11)

Our record is there as well, the struggle of one species to do more than survive, to surpass its own violent and self-concerned tendencies, its own patterns of neglect and indifference, its narrowness and divided loyalties, it's frailty and visionary promise. Like a new leaf on the tree, the fruit has not yet matured; there is trembling, an uncertain wind, a grasping of what cannot remain, the blossom falls, will the fruit be sweet or bitter? (3:12)

Mysteries of the Heart

Many are the Mysteries of the Heart!

O Blessed Spirit, how can they be recounted?
Beyond number, veiled by subtle layers
in multiple lifetimes, in uncounted relations

Mysteries of the Heart are sustained
by a great depth, by an Infinite spark that
opens to Thee, to the Fire of Illumination, to
the Eros of Transformation, to Joyfulness.

In the shadows of Thy Light, I see multitudes
each seeking a pathway toward that Light, each
carrying a torch, some fearful, some bold,
some caught in traps of anger or shame.

These mysteries are like a labyrinth, one we must
walk with courage, love, hope, and honesty
seeking the inspiration of Thy Presence, the gift
of Thy grace, the guided map of the soul.

Nature is a mystery, the heart, every creature
another revelation, every living form, a prophetic call;
the veils of the heart can be lifted, in prayer
in devotion, in love, and in abiding mutual respect.

Holy Wisdom, grant us the gift of humility, the presence
of mind, heart, and soul, to reverence all life,
to accept stewardship for Thy garden, to preserve
not destroy or deny, to love, not ignore.

*Spirit is ever-calling, vibrant in the world, only the
mirror blind us; let the transparency of Thy Presence
guide us in overcoming ignorance and empty unseeing,
so that all may abide in Thy Transparency.*

*Each on the path of the heart, each in search of
the Mysteries there concealed, each a worker
in the vineyard, each giving that they may
receive the healed heart's teachings.*

Let it be so, Holy Mother, now and always!

To Remember Spirit (4)

The challenge of the flesh is to remember Spirit, the challenge
of Spirit is to remember soul, and soul must find harmony with
flesh, all three necessary for the finding of the Other. This Other
is the Beloved, Holy Mother Spirit, Mother of Revelation, the
Source whose freedom nurtures us within the Other, to Love and
Be Loved in the cycle of all love's relations, to be the Other within
the Holy Spirit Mother, Holy Beloved, Wholly Other, Holy, Holy,
Blesséd Mother. (4:1)

I remember Spirit, in dreams and visions seen, uplifted and
carried by the over-currents into Light, into depths, into darkness
with its soothing Mysteries and Abyss, into the swirling seas of
Oceanic Being. My flesh was a garment of silk wrapped about an
energy whose inner transformation left me shocked in immobility;
early there was fear, then came wonder, in the middle period,
multitudes of dying and being reborn, a sameness purged, joy
rediscovered, a calm and stillness. (4.2)

Then came the rising of Holy Mother Spirit, like a bright star on
a lucid evening when the light has not yet faded. There is promise
in that bright astral jewel, a spectral emanation whose core is so hot
as to dissolve flesh into its primal energies of life, into the plasmic
emanations of soul-expanded being, blowing away the ashes of

fear, doubt, hope, and desire for the pure extensiveness of an all-enfolding Love, holy beyond expression. (4.3)

To remember Spirit is not simply to know Presence, but to embody Presence, to be a Keeper of the Sacred Flame, a living witness, a blesséd acolyte, an *akolouthos* (hearer) follower of the Holy Mother Spirit, dedicated to the being that is you reflecting Her in the holiness of an unending sacred work, to manifest Presence in the daily actions of thoughts, speech, deeds, and promises, to Be that Lamp to which the glass adds its luster to a lucid brilliance. (4.4)

This Lamp, this glass, this body, this individual being, is the worthy instrument of a special task, to bring light and illumination for the seeing of the world, the heavens, the interconnected Beingness of the great Expanse, the small joys that are a reflection of the astral gem, a facet in a smile, a tear, a prayer, a tiny spark that warms the Heart, a listening that hears, a touch that heals, a giving that asks no return, a clarity that reveals a hurt, a kindness freely received. (4.5)

The oil of the burning lamp, of purest olive with the fragrance of myrtle, from east and west, from north and south, from dawn and twilight, from noon and deepest night, from the rounding circle of the world, is an offering, a life source gift given so we may not stumble, nor grasp, nor take unseeming hold of our ideas, thoughts, or beliefs, but rather, to be illumined in that Presence, a Light offered without expectation, a clear, pure, radiance of generous love. (4.6)

Blesséd is the power of the Blesséd Mother Spirit! Those blessings cannot be contained, they flow like subtle liquid fire through the nerves and muscles and organs of embodied flesh, they extend out into the etheric field, they become shaping currents of astral energies, signals in the subtle realms that call to us the helping spirits of our individuated paths, the devas and angelic energies of co-creation, the Holy Spirituals that intermediate and offer help. (4.7)

Blesséd is that Blessing that falls on the innocent and guilty without distinctions, and blest is the man, woman, or child who becomes a means for the transmission of those sacred energies, to heal and to reveal, to soothe and smooth the way, to manifest and coalesce the required insights of true awakening, but more blest is the one who gives blessings without thought of blessing, without efforts to bless, without preconceptions or expectations. (4.8)

And blest are the animals, the creatures of the natural world, of earth and sky and sea, who also give blessings, who transmit as the more blest, without expectation, but through an honesty and directness of being, who give without hesitation the whole of themselves in sacred regard for those they love, support, defend. They offer unrequited service, a generosity of Spirit as a testimony of the holy work; where Spirit dwells in harmony, grace abounds. (4.9)

And blest are the plants, trees, bushes, flowers, every green and growing thing, every thistle, thorn, and barb; givers of subtle energy, keepers of deeply rooted being, sentinels of time long enduring, guarded by the nature spirits, elementals, fairies, little people, the horned deities, the goddesses of river, earth, grain, and harvest. How thankful we should be for their many gifts of food, medicine, aesthetic adornment, symbolic forms, and visionary revelations. (4.10)

And blest are the mineral beings, the many gems and crystal lives of a vibrant, living cosmos, of the living sand and rock and stone, of the mounded earth whose veins are layered by organic, quasi-organic, and inorganic stratum, by the elements that give energy, color, material potential form, alchemical substance, *Materia Mater*, as a blessing to all who walk reverently on the holy earth, receiving these gifts with respectful stewardship. (4.11)

Blest by Holy Mother Spirit are the very elements of creation— wind, water, earth, and fire, astral, etheric, bioenergetic, nuclear life, every electron, proton, neutron, quark and hadron, elemental particle, spun up, down, or across, inside out or back through time, every pulsar wave, particle of cosmic radiance, graviton, subtle energy, every form of consciousness, life, being, without exception, blessed and blessed again — in Remembrance of Spirit, they are all so blest! (4.12)

Holy Spirituals (5)

Blesséd is the Holy Mother Spirit, beyond all form and formlessness, beyond and within the multi-shaped cosmos, beyond and within the imaginations of human thought or conception; She cannot be contained. Blesséd is the Holy Spirit Mother, who gives nurture, love, support to beings, who, like a mother, offers the gift of life through the pangs of birth, death, and rebirth, through the mysteries of transformation and embodied life. (5:1)

Blesséd is the Holy Spirit Mother in all Her forms and manifestations, who can know or measure them? They are beyond counting, beyond remembering, beyond knowing, yet, for each of us there is manifestation, form as the condensations of our very thoughts, desires, and dreams. Like an eagle or a dove, like a serpent or jaguar, like an angel or a deva, a divine being, She manifests in and through those forms most appropriate to our heart's call. (5:2)

Blesséd is the Spirit Holy Mother in all her formlessness, in the Cloud of Unknowing that acts as a veil over Her Potentiality, in the depths of darkness of Her Womb, the creative Ur-space uncontainable in measurable dimensions, beyond all depth, height, width, and temporal equations. Beyond the gender of Her metaphoric matrix, beyond the Light that fructifies, ferments, stimulates, arouses, and releases Her in ecstatic unity within the All (5:3)

The ground of every Holy Spiritual is a visionary ground, a seeing that holds the heart-centered energies of Presence, Infinite and Boundless, inherent within each and every being, in a radiance of reverent adoration. In its depths it cannot be fully named and in its manifestations, it is *TheaTheos*, Goddess-God, integral energies of all gendered creation, born and sustained by the dynamic joys of co-creative life, fire and water, flux and flow, fullness and the void. (5:4)

The Holy Spiritual is a flowing forth of life, vitality, and mind circulated through the subtle energies of soul, incarnate or not, for the purposes of affirmation of Its unending capacities to create. It is Presence that fills the vastness of cosmic potential with possibilities of love, understanding, insight, and inspired relationships based in an ever-widening network of soulful beings seeking to connect to the Holy Spiritual ground of all created life. (5.5)

The Holy Spiritual is your deepest desire for God, Being, Spirit, taking the forms and transforms that best lead you to its actualization in everyday life, not fixed or held in images but fluid, flowing, adaptive, yet coalescent in the moments of your realization. Blest is the one who receives such realization and more blest are those who manifest many forms, in realizations beyond realizations, in deep resolve, freely accepted, without bias for one over another. (5.6)

How It flows from form to form, through formlessness and back again, through the manifest possibilities of Holy Spiritual life and crystallizes in a specific image or in images that best constellate our personal need and aptitude, our *Ishtadeva*, our chosen god-form, Holy and Spiritual. Within and through the form is formlessness, conscious Spirit holding the image as an inspiration but not containable, not restrained, not simply imaged or formed. (5.7)

Holy is that Spiritual which thus becomes a sacred means for realizations, deeper in awakenings to Holy Spirit Other, Holy Spirit Being, Holy Spirit Mother, each a form, each uncontainable, each a sign, a *symbolicon*, whose contents cannot be articulate for the needs of rational design, nor for the unfathomed depths of poetic form, nor for exoteric lore. The Holy Spiritual is One and Many, and more than what lies between and beyond the Alpha and Omega. (5.8)

Let each person seek the form or formlessness of the Holy Spiritual that calls, in beckoning of Spirit imageries, in ecstasy and visionary dreams, in the Holy Icons of a Life vitality, the unending spiral seeking to manifest through cycles, annual rhythms, generational communal being. Our vessels of adequate form are inevitably surpassed by overflowing potency, Higher Being, the Fountain of Life, the Grail ambrosia distilled into a single tear of thankful fulfillment. (5.9)

The Holy Spiritual has many faces, masks, images, constructions, and designs tattooed onto the foreheads of procreative humanity, as signs of what is, or was, or must Be. But there is no one form or image or manifest realization best for all, nor suitable for even a single teaching; there is only the Holy Spiritual that calls you, the Seeker, open to the creative possibility of all images and forms, received with reverence, metamorphic, transformative, unfixed. (5.10)

Many of the archetypes or Aeons of traditional religions are Holy Spirituals, Yeshu'a, Mary, Buddha, Krishna, Lao-tzu, Guan Yin, Amaterasu, the archangels and high spirits the world over, all representing and expressing Presence in unique forms and qualities of that transmit the sacred. These forms are transformational, able to sustain identity for eons but also able to shift appearances, adapt, conform, or break an old mold for a nuance not yet seen, a dynamic form not fixed or unchanging. (5.11)

The Holy Mother Spirit is also a Holy Spiritual, a living Presence of divine feminine form, not alone, nor greatest, not above or below other forms or formlessness, not reducible to a creed or code or teaching, but a true Holy Spiritual, an uncontainable Image, a Mystery imaged in a multitude of forms, words, thoughts, not held in gender's sway, but Wisdom beyond male or female, a nurturing Presence, like a Mother, like a Lover, like a Woman divinely blessed—like, like—not IS. (5.12)

Uncontainable Desire (6)

There is a deep and uncontainable desire in the heart of every creature to know Source and Origin, to know purpose and end, to know the path by which a conscious being attains deeper fullness, a vital resonance with the energies of individual existence, harmony with others that sustains in ever widening waves, the interconnected circles of multiple life-forms, nurtured by the Source of All That Is. (6:1)

For many, this desire is obscure, lost in the struggle and comforts of living, lost in heartbreaks, sorrows, wounds or conflictual relations, fallen into the shadow lands of sleeping sensibilities caught in patterns of social expectation, trapped in striving after goals that do not fulfill deep soul desire, that subverts, deflects, and redirect energies toward ends that leave only a residue of insight shoring up a tired life, complacent or forgetful. (6:2)

The energies of aspiration are born of this uncontainable desire, to embrace life, to engage and interact, to be affirmed, accepted, admired, or loved; the germination of this seed-desire takes many forms, can mutate into variations less healthy or less well rooted in fertile soil. The deep roots of this desire draw vitality from the earth, expands awareness through absorbed Light that soul may flower in all the colors of its hidden potentiality. (6.3)

This desire needs guidance, intentional commitment for its satisfaction, a well lived life concurrent with its fulfilled realizations; it is a desire of soul, not of mind or body, but of the deeper self, where the vitality of life-awareness overflows the vessel of the heart, uplifted by a pure and sacred Presence. We are called to this realization—that the uncontainable desire, the urge for spiritual wisdom, be fulfilled in holy living. (6.4)

As the heart opens to this desire, feels the depth and fullness of its calling, there is a realization that dawns—a recognition that this deep desire lies in others, lighting the path that leads to compassion, loving kindness, and respect. It is a call to Holy Being, to the work of transformation, to an awakening that unites us with that call within each incarnate soul, differentiated but resonant with deep love and appreciation. (6.5)

I have been called, along with others, to this work of soul

awakening, to the Mystery of Emergence, to inner purifications and the Sacred Work of holy distillation, to the ecstatic embrace of the Holy Mother Spirit, to the rose water sweetness and the sparkling diadem that signifies a blesséd grace—in scent, sight, sound, taste, touch, and motion, in prescient revelations, in prophetic dreams, in the still, quiet Voice. (6.6)

In dreams and visions, in conscious insight, this desire seeks deepening satisfactions, a fuller knowledge that can bestow a benediction, a resurrection of soul, from its worldly preoccupations to more centered, spiritual concerns. The desire is soul-rooted and cannot be satisfied with simple conformity to norms and values that do not emerge, or extend beyond the given, or reach past the boundary of convention and tradition. (6.7)

What is good is preserved, what is an affirmation of life-vitality and growing, glowing health, is carried from form to form, image to image, through ongoing transformations which cannot hold the fullness in any lesser desire. Uncontainable means ever seeking, growing, transmuting, through solar, lunar, astral, planetary cycles, to more inclusive, complex, and intra-linked relations, all seeking passionate, harmonic realizations. (6.8)

This desire, this primal urge, has great emotional intensity, infuses itself into the mental life of the most holy, elevates mind to new visions, carries lovers to ecstasy, and provides an energetic core, a pulsar of vibrant passion whose fulfillment is ever opening to new horizons of insight, emotional maturity, and ethical concern. Its energies are those of pure creation, sustaining deep and undiminished self-aware expression. (6.9)

This urgency of Spirit, this overflowing fullness that will not be contained, this constant breaking of vessels that are then reformed to hold a fuller measure, is the very nature of developing Life, Health, and Well-Being; it is the Holy Mother Spirit flowing into and through forms that cannot contain but only shape or mold a possible content whose meaning does not include All Beings, all conditional values, all absolutes. (6.10)

This desire is multifoliate, a rose whose petals cannot be counted, a hermetic emblem of inner potency lost or denied in hollow living; the bell rings and its vibrant echoes spread in waves of holy sound but among the hurrying crowd, many do not hear, do not respond, do not care to heed its call, acknowledge its power, or joy, or potency that would challenge conformity, known symbolisms, resistant static truths. (6.11)

Holy Mother Spirit, hear me! Your vitality is a pure fountain of lucid energies flowing with life into every living creature, embodied or not, as generative and regenerative Presence lifting us beyond the held horizon of belief or thought! Inspire us with the courage to reach beyond our own limitations, to accept with humility our deeper possibilities, and with joy, to embrace the desire for overflowing fullness! (6.12)

Giving Thanks

Blessed Spirit Mother, guide our thoughts, our desires,
our inclinations toward Light,

Guide us to that Depth of Inner Solitude where
we can give thanks for the Gift of Life,

May the blessings of Your Presence flow forth
to all those seeking Inspiration,

To all those whose prayers and desires lead to
a greater love, sharing, caring, and hope,

Hear the silent words of every heart desiring life,
guide those souls to incarnate awakenings,

Receive the sorrows of all those who have suffered
and nurture them with renewal.

We give thanks for Your gifts, Your blessings, for
the many graces you have given us,

We give thanks for health, awareness, intelligence, for
love, sharing, kindness, and humor,

We give thanks for Your Presence, Wisdom, Illuminations
flowing forth from the All, to be received by Many.

Holy Mother Spirit, guide our thoughts and prayers,
lead us to understanding without confusion

Show us the Path and the Way, that we might walk
with dignity, toward the Unseen.

That we might See

That we might Be!

The Path and the Way (7)

There is no One Path or One Way, only a multitude of Paths, all leading to different ends and to various goals that may coalesce or be distinct and unique. The Way has no one articulation other than the relative and finite truths we actually embody and the Path has many branches, side tracks, and different consequences; but all these diverse teachings are harmonized in the deep practice of kindness, love, and peaceful co-creative respect. (7.1)

Where is the teaching that would satisfy all diverse humanity? Where is the path that all would take and that no one would renounce or abandon? There is no such teaching and no such path; but there are words and thoughts of wisdom, there is insight that offers light and guidance, there is a hopeful multitude that would join energies in co-creative life, seeking to better comprehend the over-flowing Fullness. (7.2)

The Path of the Heart is one such Way, and the Path of Wisdom is another; the Path of Humility without attachment to rewards, a third; Service in healing and aid to others yet a fourth; and there is a Fifth Path, the Path of Mystery and Inspiration based on the gifts of Spirit as given by the Holy Mother Presence. This Fifth Path has many forms, in art, in science, in religions, in quiet words, in stillness, in deep calm. (7.3)

The Path of the Heart is a deep soul-centered Way, it is found in many teachings, among the Sufi, the Christian Mystics, the Bhakti of India, in Jewish Kabbalah, in the compassion of the Buddha, in the tears of Jesus, in the love of a mother for her child. The energies of soul expand outward to encompass and meet the soul expanse of others; in the subtle energies a resonance is formed, a vibrancy reflected in the leaf and flower of all we love. (7.4)

The Path of Wisdom is deep, unfathomable, a luminosity of unspeakable insights sustained in Spirit, Holy Mother Light, Holy Father Dark, an alchemical marriage of opposites whose differences are not dissolved. There is unity but also diversity, oneness but also a multiplicity, differentiated forms, a plenitude of living beings whose uniqueness is the greatest gift, whose individual nature is a Jewel in the Net of Co-Creation. (7.5)

The Path of Humility is the one that comes after, not before, from behind, not in front, last, but not least; a path that does not seek to validate a claim of superiority in insight or understanding, in love or service, in kindness or forgiveness. Letting-go and hanging-on are left behind, there is simply being-present without judgment, a Path of Non-Grasping, deep acceptance of the Way — what comes, comes; what goes, goes; all between Is that which Is. (7.6)

The Path of Service has no end; it is a constant working for the betterment of others, self, all; it is not selfless, nor is it passive; not a lack of skill but an expertise in bringing forth that which cries out to be born. The Holy Mother Spirit is the birth-spark, each of us, the mid-wife, the attendant, the physician of soul's forthcoming; energy, work, effort, sweat, and tears are required, courage, fortitude, determination, commitment to serve is the challenge. (7.7)

I found the Fifth Path without seeking, it came unannounced, often at night, in the stillness of the Hermetic Hour, before dawn, a herald of what is yet to come; it grasped me in dreaming visions, did not ask permission nor give direction, it simply swept me up into vast horizons and said to me, in the silence of soul's language, "Behold! You, a mortal, are also immortal, asleep, and must awaken from your dreaming mind to see and be what Is and what Must Become." (7.8)

The energies of that Path, the awakenings, descents and ascents, transformations, and encounters cannot be held within the boundaries of only soul's expansion and contraction; they reach out beyond the known and open to the Unknown, a Becoming, to offer soul a true Beholding in brilliant light, in depths of darkness, in twilight and dawn, the spiral of evolving, galactic life. So much life! Each life so rare, so precious, so vast, so interconnected through the All. (7.9)

The Fifth Path is the Path of your personal awakening, the Path of your love and inspiration realized in direct participation, in the immediacy of the Holy Mother guiding your fulfillment through activities of soul overflowing, with Presence and Joy, with Beauty in Wholeness singing. Like the softness of the moon's purity, an amber glow, a rainbow of colors whose palette holds all shades and whose strokes softly paint the images of your desire. (7.10)

Blessed is the Path and the Way, beyond the known, that we may know more fully the possibilities of all paths and ways. The Path of Paths is a way, of the heart, mind, and soul, of humility and service, of wisdom, compassion, and love. It is not limited by the thoughts of a founder, nor by the goals of its dreamers and visionaries; it is a Path of Surrender, a willing acceptance of maturity without presuppositions, guided by lucid clarity, a union of Soul and Spirit. (7.11)

Mind must take responsibility, heart must feel with empathy the joys and sorrows of the world, memory must be keen and alert, foresight a purity of intuition, will an active and flexible energy of response, body a temple that soul may shine forth, in breath, the luster of sacred Presence. Guide our thoughts, Holy Mother Spirit, our intentions, relationships, memories of the departed, reverence for Life, our prescient knowing of Thy Being, ever Active and Aware! (7.12)

Deepest Ground of Being (8)

I rarely use the word "God" as it does not have the resonance of the Infinite free from dogma and theological presuppositions. All God words have limits imposed by the beliefs of the believer and, in my own mind, there are limits as well. In traditional teachings which emphasize the superiority or blessedness of their teachings over the traditions of others, there is too much limitation; like a temple that will only accept elect and right-thinking persons. (8.1)

But all people, all beings, all animate creatures of all space and time are inseparable from the universal Temple, the multidimensional Cosmos. And the thoughts and beliefs of men, constructed through institutions, hierarchies, political ambitions, and patriarchal authority cannot contain the reality that is God. I do not call it God, I call it Deepest Ground of Being, Holy Mother Spirit is its active energies, all beings are the vessels of its manifestations. (8.2)

There is no measuring this Deepest Ground, no enumerating its qualities, no description that is adequate to its unfathomable depths and fullness. It is beyond Infinite and allows the Infinite to be its shadow, its archetype of immeasurability. It is Deep within each being, the *Bythos* of individual, collective, and species life; nor is it simply within, for the depths of soul resonate, responding to a music of spheres, a harmony of knowing, an all-inclusive inner-outer-beyond Unity. (8.3)

It is not the Zero-Point Field, for this field, lacking consciousness in theories of energy and matter cannot represent its sacred capacity for Life and its power for creation in existences, diverse and subtle. Nor is it Void, Empty, Non-Existent, yet it contains all of these in the capacities that human beings have for self-negation and abandonment of What Is. It is a More that has no lack, a Most that has no loss, a Best that accepts the Better as Its own Good. (8.4)

The Deepest Ground of Being, like the ocean of all becoming, is something more than a field or a quantum effect; something other than the bound energies of all particles, molecules, compounds, and electro-plasmic fluids found in the vast reaches of space both great and very small. It is Depth out of which mind, soul, awareness, intelligence, love, empathy, telekinetic synchronicity, hyper-consciousness evolves to explore the Depths of our connectedness. (8.5)

There is no place and no time where this Depth of Being is

not; no timeless, atemporal horizon that is not sustained by Its omnipresent vitality and living sentience, call it Divine Abundance, call it Everlasting, Immortal Joy. Seek it in your own Heart, in your memory of lives past and future, in the play of consciousness scripted for cycle upon cycle of evolving interaction, in the hurricane and quiet rain, in the sunset, in dawn, in the twilight before new life and insight. (8.6)

It is there in Death and in Rebirth, in the sustaining harmony that provides the context for transition between worlds, states, levels, dimensions, and hyper-alternatives. It is there in the matrix of every thought and feeling, in the muscles of your body, the cells of your brain, the chemistry of your perceptions, the wavicles of your transubstantiations. Yet, it is irreducible, cannot be held in chemistry or bone, the electromagnetic aura, or in causal thought. (8.7)

It is a true Mystery, a Holy Reality, a Deepest Ground whose energies, thoughts, perceptions, actions, or pragmatic creations are all instrumentalized through the diverse species of all worlds, planes, cosmoi, and galactic megaforms. The subtle gossamer Entirety which lives in the dew of the morning grass is its incarnation, as is the volcano and the nebular cloud seen by living beings on a thousand worlds; Mystery within Mysteries, Labyrinths of Being. (8.8)

I cannot comprehend God, I cannot grasp or understand that Depth but I have a sense of It, an intuitive and mystical perception of Presence, a psychic awareness that expands into the vastness and then brings me back to the shelter of my body, to the arms of my beloved, to the quiet of my home, my friends, my location in the matrix of incarnate space, held like a candle flame against a wind immeasurable in strength but overflowing with life and love. (8.9)

Blesséd is the Immeasurable Depths of the Holy Ground, the living matrix whose energies are woven in the fabric of space-time as constellated in mandalas of collective life that extend over many worlds, many suns, moons, planets, stars and in transient bursts of slow awakening to true communion. Blesséd are our sister and brother worlds, our mother and father worlds, our child worlds, sheltered and nurtured by the Holy Ground. (8.10)

Holy Mother Spirit, guardian of the blessing light, keeper of the flame, nurture our wisdom and maturity in opening to that Deep Ground, to the subconscious soul as it awakens, step by step, to the living, animate universe of all collective Life. May the Great Mandala of World Realization, in whose form all religions, traditions, and teaching offer the sweetness of their insights, unfold like a golden flower, a pure lotus of luminous, radiant Wisdom. (8.11)

Every creation is a God, every being, a God in the process of Becoming, through the Deepest Ground of Being, through the inner realization of its inmost possibility. But then, we go beyond God or Gods or Goddesses into the something Other that is still Us, into the Mystery of the More Than God that preserves our wisdom, drops the form to find the evolving Essence, the Infinite that propagates diversity in harmonies of Being no longer bound by What Was. (8.12)

Illusions and Illuminations (9)

Not all mystical visions lead to insight, not all illumination produce wisdom, some can mislead, some create illusions, and some are only a substitute expressing immaturity. The goal is not mystical visions; the goal is to live with humility and kindness based on a deep knowledge of incarnate life, gained through compassion and the sharing of insights. Life is a deep river with many tributaries, knowing the ocean does not necessarily mean knowing the river. (9.1)

Illusion is to take the image, as in a mirror, for the reality, to take the vision for truth, to take the mystical insight for an absolute. In the Sea of Becoming, there are no final absolutes, only currents and convections made by the turning world, by the light of mind and the cool depths of soul. Spirit is the medium of understanding, the current that keeps us afloat and guides us through the cycles of death and rebirth for the good of all, not simply for one good. (9.2)

There are many diverse teachings, realizations, insights, and paths; all offer alternatives to conception, and perspectives on transformations, and no one path is absolute, final, finished. There is no end but going-on creative discovery, our possible fulfillment in the deep potential of soul inspired actions, our collective and individuated searches for greater wisdom. Truth lies at the intersection, the crossroads of many paths, in multiple rays of realization. (9.3)

If I dream at the center, in the Holy Light of an Infinite Ocean, in Being and Mystery, then I behold the source of Illumination; but when I wake from that vision, I must bring its vitality into the world of thinking, feeling, acting others, who may not share the vision or the dream. Thus, the task is not simply a recitation of What Is, but a call to understand What Has Not Yet Become; it is a calling of soul to the work of translation, to the interpretive challenge that makes real the possible. (9.4)

But visionary insight is like a forest not yet cultivated by human intentions for the purpose of settlement; we are seekers after pathways, called to the future to reconcile the ancient past with new understandings. I do not abide in settlement but in discovery and exploration of the possible, in the making of signs for those who come after, in the painting of images whose contents are subversions of normal everydayness, openings to the extraordinary, revealing the Unseen. (9.5)

There are no limits to illumination and no goal that is an adequate testimony to the diversity of all possible insights; we do not follow a single path toward a known end, but a plurality whose center is Infinite while Ever One. Finding the Center, knowing it and marking a pathway, is a contribution to its multiplicity, a gift given that others may follow. But knowing it also means knowing the limits of the illumination, its boundaries and edge. (9.6)

These illuminations, as gifts of Spirit, are sources of our

awakening, given to us as inspired realizations uplifting us toward greater heights, drawing us down into the creative dark, balancing us between the Infinite within and without. Blessed are those who attain illumination and more blessed those whose teaching are a guide to other; but most blessed are those who have gone beyond illumination into the perfect harmony of the within, the without, and the All. (9.7)

Knowledge is limited by the paradigms of our thoughts, dreams, intuitions, and empathic relations; it is not infinite nor does it reach, even in mystical realizations, the fullness that is the Deeper Ground of Being. We want to possess the Infinite but we are led by the illusions of enlightenment toward a bound horizon that cannot hold the Beauty and Bounty of the truly Vast; thus, we offer in Its place, conceptual absolutes, or simple Emptiness. (9.8)

Our paradigms of knowledge must grow beyond fixed forms and unchanging imaginings, the dynamic core is the fire-rose that illumines the heart but does not remain unchanging, indicating a depth of fullness that continues to overflow the boundaries of our imaginal constructions. Rather than Absolutes, let us embrace an ever-evolving Continuity that builds, stage by stage, toward new discoveries, new forms, adaptive to our growing maturity and wisdom. (9.9)

There is a deep Wisdom that participates in All That Is, that is able to abide in the flux and flow of the deepest currents, with perfect transparency, perfect harmony of grace, in the fullness of the All that Becomes. It is a rare and special Wisdom, a golden white lotus whose subtle emanations of the heart have no boundaries, and whose self is an image able to dissolve into the current and to flow without obstruction, in perfect freedom, adaptive and creatively responsive. (9.10)

Blest are those who attain this Wisdom but more blest are those who are able to incarnate the qualities of that Wisdom in application to all teachings and all pathways, without clinging to either name or form. There is no Buddhism, no Daoism, no

Advaita, no Sufism, no Kabbalah, no Mystical Christ-Spirit that lacks this Wisdom when all pathways dissolve into the heart of radiance beyond paths, schools, and traditions, beyond words and thoughts. (9.11)

Do not call it empty or void, those are words and forms of formlessness; do not call it absolute or relative; do not call it higher or lower; do not call it by the name of any path, but call it in prayer, in silence, in love and holding, call it in the sunset and dawn of spiritual awakenings, call it through loved others, through gentleness, generosity, humility, kindness, abundance of vitality, through grace, compassion, joy in giving and receiving, through the many harmonies of true lucid Wisdom. (9.12).

Blessed Mother Spirit

Our joy is incomplete without Thy Love,
Our love is incomplete without Thy Joy.

Our longing is a sacred search for Thee
Thy longing is a sacred making of the We.

Mother, there is no Mystery deeper
than the holiness of Thy Sea; all the oceans
in boundless symphony cannot
match the clarion call of Thy
Blessed Infinity.

Guide us to safe harbor, open to Thy Sea,
to a place of refuge from which we may
explore the yet unknown shore.

Draw us into the currents of Thy Love
and guide us to new horizons yet unseen
that we may become all the more.

Open our longing soul to Thy rhythms
in ecstatic dance, to trance, to advance
toward the glowing light of Thy
ever splendid Grace.

The Light of that Sea is every star,
the sun, moon, planets, tides of space,
phosphorescent with life in all forms,
aware beings deeply seeking love.

Mother, Daughter, Virgin, Child
your smile is in my heart, your song on my lips,
your taste like honey, a nectar of soul received
in the kiss of Thy Beloved Presence!

Grant us wisdom, O Sophianic Light!

Let the Father, Son, Boy, and Man
stand with You, partnered in love through
Thy Grace, in a place without shame
To embrace Thy Holy Name.

Love, may you never depart my soul!

Blessed Mother, make us whole, complete
through the Mystery of Thy loving grace.

So be it, now and always.

Amen

Logosophic Inspirations (10)

Words upon words, stacked and shuffled and parsed with ever finer precision even as the meanings disappear; a locust cloud of words covering the delicate membranes of the glowing world, obscuring sacred intent, heavy with explanation. The *hieros logoi* (sacred words), the signatures of the Mystery inscribed on human hearts, are buried beneath the onslaught of words; yet, even there, amidst words, there are glimmering strands, light threads of connected meaning, weaving a charismatic pattern for those who can see. (10.1)

Inspiration does not come unbidden but bubbles up from the soul-well when heart and mind connect, in the dance, with Spirit Ever-Living, in a flow of sounds that sing the world from imagined subtle forms into vibrant articulate Being, into poetic songs, prayers, forms, dream narratives meant to shape alternate realities, giving birth without fear of censure or blame. Free words of truth cannot be elected by consent but must sail where the winds of Spirit blow, as Logosophy, wisdom words. (10.2)

I have sought words all my life as vehicles for sharing, *medias res*, in the midst of the action, my groping after a single rare moment of expression, when Spirit will shine through the morass of my own limitations, overpower my clumsy attempts at expression, and reveal a breathless moment of grace, woven in the text and texture of an unseen but now expressed perception, one imbued with joy by the brilliance of the subtle world revealed. (10.3)

Hidden behind words, is the Wisdom we aspire to, the fire that lights the horizon with undiscovered meaning meant to illumine, to give solace and guidance in alleyways and dark corners, to be a clarion call of awakening, to see, to behold, to open the eyes of inward vision to the sacred harmonies of sight, sound, touch, and feeling speech. Words are only gateways to insight, only a subtext that points beyond itself, arrows speeding toward the blooming, glowing Sun. (10.4)

O Goddess of Speech, Holy Mother Spirit of the Word, Wisdom Mother, Blessed Vak of the Holy Vedas, Sophos Logoi, Prajnaparamita, Blessed Tara Green and White, let the vast energies of your creative words reconstruct the world, reshape the teachings, texts, and forms, realign the intersection of myth, meaning, and imagination to give birth to deeper guidance, soul felt direction for the recovery of holy speech and the sacred power of inner transformation. (10.5)

Let *Agape Logoi*, the "love words" of creative inspiration flow forth from the gifted hearts of a multitude of visionaries; let the blessed words of women sail beyond the islands of bound speech, past the mountains of the masculine word, into the lowlands of the fertile earth to plant there abundant forest gardens that give birth to the lungs of the world, to wind woven speech that teaches new respect, love and joy in all nature, to all creatures, to every body, mind, heart and soul. (10.6)

Let the calm, dedicated harmony of multiple voices join in choir, finding the highs and lows, the harmonic overtones, the span of musical possibility through every voice finding its proper relation to all others. In deliberate partnership, in spontaneous discovery, in unknown resonance, let voices join in a Song of Songs to articulate a lasting Wisdom for the purposes of enduring peace, creativity, and shared joy in co-creation. (10.7)

The Harmony of the Spheres is a great, subtle vibration across the spectrums of consciousness that reflects a creative potential, a possible awakening to vitality, intensity, joyful ecstasy, through an opening of the ears, through a willingness to hear a hidden thought, through an inner surrender to illumination, a willingness to be grasped, spoken through, as a nodal point, a confluence of the Holy Spiritual, a tongue of flame to light the wick of others. (10.8)

The Sophianic teachings have no form best suited to expression; all forms, genres, written text, or media may carry wisdom, and yet, Wisdom surpasses every form and cannot be reduced to lesser content. It is not content, but Presence that matters; not form, but the creative energies of Inspiration that reveals. Wisdom can be found in an elegance of mathematical expression, a perfect graft of hidden truths, in a quantified formula, or a poem. It is not form but living Spirit shining through a barely contained expression that teaches best. (10.9)

The greatest book of Wisdom is the well-lived, compassionate, exemplary life; no text is greater than the living soul embodied, holding the dignity, grace, joy, and abundance of Spirit that results in teachings worthy of memory. We remember how compassionate, forgiving, loving, joyful, humble, kind, thoughtful, responsible, exemplary were those we learned from, who taught us in the living flesh, how better to be human and embrace our sacredness. (10.10)

The greatest book is the Book of Life, the unwritten text of our desire and struggle to perfect our understanding, love, care, and concern for the world and all its creatures. The greatest teaching is by example; the greatest gift, the giving of our attention to what matters, knowing how to discard personal distractions for the embodiment of our beloved Ideals. To be wise means to live by Praxis Sophiana, to enact the highest virtues without thought of rewards; to be wise means to live wisely. (10.11)

Perfection is not the goal. We are each called to the task of Wisdom in concert with our capacity, our limitations, our embeddedness in the collective, our conditionality. Our challenge is to live with courage in search of a more fulfilled life, linked to the well-being of others, for the purposes of creative transformation. Our reward is to pass on the legacy of our learning for the good of others, doing our utmost to surpass our limits, knowing we are finite, but also knowing Holy Sophia is our guide, help, and support. (10.12)

The Golden White Lotus (11)

Symbol of the luminous heart, subtle with the energies of creation, a Sophianic image born out of the waterways of ancient Egypt; from the temple pools of India, the delicate gardens of China and Japan, to the myriad waters of the Americas, it blossoms forth in delicate array, a radiant white flower on green leaves with a golden aura of holy Presence. Call it the *Raa-Nub*, golden light, the signature of divinity, a sacred sign, inscribed on the heart through a creative act of Imagination and Devotion. (11:1)

Envision this Golden White Lotus shining in your heart, its golden light penetrating your aura, extending into the subtle domain, into the ParaUniverse, into etheric realms, its roots drawing sustenance from your embodied life, the fine tendrils drawing vitality from the very Ground of Incarnational Being. Through roots and nerves and channels of Chi, through the *Brahma nādī*, the *prāna* flows, 72,000 channels of light illumine your aura. (11:2)

Behold the Goddess dwelling within the Lotus, Holy Mother

Spirit, infinite in form and kind; behold Her perfect union with the God-Light of the heart; be the alchemical ecstasy, the infusion of the one into the other until there is no difference, no distinction, no separation. And yet, from this union, a thousand souls are born, the universe recreated, time and space made possible, the unmanifest manifest, and the possibility of individual life made real. (11:3)

A Christ manifestation gave me the Raa-Nub, inscribed in a book, drawn at the bottom of its title page, and years passed before I comprehended, before I was able to fathom its depthless meanings, before I realized it was an alchemical sign, a union of Father Sun and Mother Cow, of Raa and Hathor, of heaven and earth, of male and female, of light and dark, sun and milk, all permeated by the Third, a sweet honey butter of Presence, churned into gold, luminous drops of Presence, spun from the Infinite, a sweet ecstasy of Taste. (11:4)

The sages of India say the *Anahata Chakra*, lotus wheel of the heart, has twelve pedals, and every lotus is different pedaled for each center in the body; I have not seen this, nor made such fine discriminations. I see only the form and its light, its roots, green leaves, white pedals, and its golden center; the luminous aura extends, expands, encompasses, nourished by clear visualization, empowered by Presence, radiant from the heart, utterly alive. (11.5)

The Heart Lotus births other lotus forms, each manifesting at the various centers, a chain of lotus flowers, strung on the *Brahma nādī*, the God-channel, the central core of the spine, from base to brain, culminating in the Lotus of the Eighth Center, three finger widths above the head. There it floats, an empathic Lotus link, both sign and signal, brilliant with its message of awareness, a higher orb of light within the aura, sending out and receiving, resonant with the gift of grace. (11.6)

The Golden White Lotus is a sign of purity, an image of renunciation, not attained through denial of the body but through the shedding of tears, through giving up all selfishness and harm to others, through casting off doubt, fear, rage, hate, denial, all arrogance, through a deep purity of intent to live without harm or injury to others, with humility, devotion, responsible care, and resonant love, to purify the mind, the body, the heart, the will, and our hopes. (11.7)

The Golden White Lotus is a sign of joy and ecstasy, an opening of the closed bud, a flowering forth stimulated by the rising Sun; soothed and shrouded in the pale glow of moonlight, it awakens as the Dawn of Presence. The Sun of ever-conscious Light acts upon our meditation, enlivens the image, quickens the flow from root to leaf, spreads the pedals of heart to new openings, to a soft reception of Spirit, liquid essence elixir, sweet on the tongue of the soul. (11.8)

The Golden White Lotus is a means, a conjunction of will, imagination, and mind to set the image within as psychic nexus; fusion of beauty, sensitivity, delicacy, pure in form and color, dense with meanings of past, present, and future. Whoever reads the sign complete, sees the path beyond the labyrinth, traverses the forest signs, attains the hill of vision, beholds the dawning light, and dissolves all form into an Ocean far beyond imagining. (11.9)

The path of the Golden White Lotus is a spiral out into the Vastness of all Creation and a spiral inward toward an Infinite Depth; it is a ritual dance in rhymed rhythm, a charisma of caring based in the double motion of inwardness conjoined with all-inclusiveness, a synthesis that dissolves the distinction between inner and outer, yet leaves a trace, a transparent sense of integrity, will, action as the creative expression of individuality conjoined within the All. (11.10)

The Golden White Lotus is a form of prayer, a meditation on the living cosmos embodied in holy beauty, an envisioned offering of the heart to the All Creator, a flower offered at the altar of Love for the purpose of transformation, a gift given as an emblem of change held in clasped hands, head bowed or eyes closed, breath regulated and deep, mind still as the lucid lotus pond, a silent offering of the heart that Light may awaken the sleeping soul. (11:11)

Blesséd is the power of Imagination, the gift that liberates us from the bound life of tradition, authority, and paternalism; blesséd is the capacity to see the unseen, to create with imagery, sound, and feeling, the emergent, undiscovered powers of soul for the purpose of inspired growth; and most blesséd is every soul who uses this power for the betterment of the world, all her creatures, and every soul without defilement, impurity, or false purposes. (11.12)

The Pan-Sentient Cosmos (12)

There is a Hermetic teaching, *Hen to Pan*, "the One that is All" representing a unified cosmos of beings engaged in creative processes of becoming. When we examine that *logion* carefully, we see the All is a deeply sentient All, not a material cosmos, not just energies and mass, but a living ocean of beings interacting with intelligible purpose and desires. It is a sentient cosmos, an All that reverberates with life, awareness, and response, a place of Mystery and Being, a becoming that never ends. (12.1)

It is a Mystery because we do not comprehend its origin or purpose, we speculate and imagine, study and theorize, but we do not know, only believe and act in accord with that belief. I believe this cosmos, this psycho-spatial order, is sentient all the way down, right into the smallest bits and strings, into its multidimensional currents replete with sentient capacities. These capacities are basic—attraction, repulsion, neutrality—the three fundamental qualities of sentience; core attributes of Being. (12.2)

In the simplest forms, these three attributes seek coordination, like to like, in an increasing tableau of emergent forms, strings, particles, quarks and gluons, atoms, molecules, advancing into ever more complex forms. Attraction and repulsion become norms of organization, neutrality a medium of openness that allows forms to evolve in accord with the animating sense of the Whole. The Whole is there, a primary given, the One that is All, always present, a Birth Mother of all Becoming. (12.3)

Sentience evolves, it does not simply appear complete, only

as process, a becoming that requires billions of years, millions of eons, to create the miracle of sentience self-awareness. This becoming requires complexity, an emergence that requires endless cycles of trial and error, of gradual and sudden *gestalten*, forming patterns and then dissolving into other forms, a stochastic process of discovery seeking stability in actual entities through creative realizations that can endure. (12.4)

In this process, time is duration, not measurable nor lineal, but cyclical and patterned by cycles that embrace the tempos of seasonal change, ecological contexts, embeddedness in dynamic transformations moving only as rapidly as sentience needs; a turning world, a rising and setting sun and moon, sea tides and cloud formations, hyperstatic discharge and disequilibrium leading to new synthesis and harmonic balances. A world and cosmos in process, becoming, reactive, alive. (12.5)

As sentience evolves, awareness increases beyond the three primaries, into a slow complexity of responses as needs and desires form, aspirations, goals, striving, but also hurt, resistance, avoidance, caution, and a sense of danger. In this growth process soul comes into Being, not as made but as evolved, a slowly growing awareness of change, new patterns, possibilities, and ways of becoming, attuned to place, locale, biogenic conditions, inherited tendencies, emergent creative possibilities. (12.6)

This soul-becoming is slow, eons in evolution, only slowly reaching the threshold of self-awareness, only over generations, waking up to the very fact of awareness. In this waking, as Hermetic discovery, soul takes on its own life, able to survive bodily death, able to continue its cycles of learning and discovery. The old communal soul life is surpassed, the oceanic life of shared consciousness slowly dissolves, becomes in many stages, individualized, over thousands of cycles, a slow birthing of soul awareness. (12.7)

I once had a vision of this past, I was taken back into the formative ages where individuation had not yet occurred, where I could see the merged communal mindedness of the primordial sea, afloat with simple life forms sharing awareness in the most primal sense. I watched the changing evolution, how sentience evolved slowly allowing for partitions, organic distinctions, new life forms, no longer strictly communal, giving birth to differentiated groups, species distinctions, deeply sharing awareness. (12.8)

Over many cycles of duration, these differentiations became more distinctive, forming cultural patterns through communal sharing and group actions; soul was growing, evolving, slowly becoming self-aware, no longer unified by undercurrents of consensual norms or attitudes. Beliefs differentiated, soul individualized, self-awareness was enhanced, complexity led to emergence, new understanding arising, mythically structured and communally embedded, music, dance, art, philosophy appeared. (12.9)

All was utterly sentient, from the simplest particle to the most complex expressions of awareness, sentience was the ground and source, the medium of development fostered by the One that was All, the unitary Infinite whose core sentience gave constant birth to new becoming through new insights and new embodiments. This holy ground permeated all, becoming more evident in the perceptions of discreet individuals and groups that celebrated the ancient truth, all is alive, the entire universe is pan-sentient miracle, sentient throughout, a living cosmos of creative Being. (12.10)

We are born, *medias res*, in the midst of the action, the past obscure and the future unknown, we struggle to put the puzzle of existence into a meaningful pattern, and yet, the Whole abides, supports us, nurtures creativity, providing a vast reservoir of insights, writing, teachings, and practices to assist our personal awakening to Spirit and Mystery. The Pan-Sentient cosmos is the living, vital, dynamic, energetic source of this becoming, we need only open our minds to its vast, inspiring resources. (12.11)

The Pan-Sentient universe is one in which life is primary, not secondary and not derivative, but fully and utterly fundamental, from the earliest moment, through all stages of evolution, these are the primaries: energy, matter, sentience, spirit, the Whole. They are, were, and ever-shall-be, present, interdependent, co-relational, and inseparable from all the deep capacities we have for spiritual transformation. We embrace all primaries, thankful that in a complex universe of becoming we can recognize them as such. (12.12)

PART TWO

Luminous Father, Heavenly Light

May the living stars illumine Thy
deep interior, Father of Lights!

May the darkest depths of Heaven
reveal the presence of Life in all Invisible
forms in the swirl of a cosmic nebulae, in
the blasted matter-light of intersected stars,
in the vibrant energies of world inhabiting souls.

May the spermatakoi, Your living seeds, find
fertile soil, birthing in partnership, in the womb
of transplanetary space, the ageless miracle
of a seeded world, pregnant with
Source Life.

May our sensory perceptions behold
the unexpected vision of life among the stars
like musical notations, a scale of being
that permutates into uncountable harmonies
creating context upon context for
joyful, emergent Life.

May the Father of Lights, the collective unitary
Mind of all stellar and astral forms,
unveil our limited awareness for a vaster
Presence in which soul sings ecstatically,
in resonance, with all living creatures
near and far, brother-sisters of
an Infinite Horizon.

And may the desiring soul of every individual,
each hallowed life-form, find its Way, find
the path that leads beyond the confines
of its acquired knowledge for
a deepening of the roots
by which knowledge
is given and
received
Amen

*

So be it, Now and Always!

The Sacred Human (13)

It is not only the human that is called sacred, all life is sacred, and the entire cosmos is alive, throbbing with theophanic Presence, radiant with the energies of Ever-Living Spirit. What makes the human sacred is our capacity to recognize the sacredness within all, that every living creature is a gift, a treasure, a unique offering from the Womb of Creation. The obligation of this recognition is reverence for all life and a call to nurture its stages, however ferocious, strange, or other the forms in which it manifests. (13.1)

The sacred human is a path of discovery, an unveiling of a deep potential as we learn to walk in balance with other life, with a multitude of creatures great and small; a centered walk from which comes a dawning realization, an opening of the heart to the joy of mutuality and partnership. This is not a path of dominance or caretaking but a profound realization of partnership, of serving the needs of the disinherited, the liminal, remnants of a once fertile, abundant diversity collapsing under confused, hostile, uncertain human anxieties, fears, and arrogance. (13.2)

The discovery of the sacred human cannot occur in isolation from all earthly life; we must honor the gift of species diversity for it is the rare, precious, hard to find gift of a living world rampant with unique life forms and marvelous, intricate beauties and blinding colors marking each individual form. The striped albino tiger, the macaw, the fire ant, the coral snake, the bee and spider, winged creatures, wood stalkers, grass eaters, swimmers, or earth crawlers—every life deserves our greatest care, love, and utmost support. (13.3)

We humans are not unique as living beings, we are but one form among a million million, yet every form is sacredness embodied, every life interdependent, connected through living streams of life-source energy, Spirit-filled, animate with sentience that cannot be measured or ranked. The depths of this sentience are Infinite, a capacity that takes a universe to manifest, all time and all space; this world is but one, many others will become known, but each rare, a miracle of abundance contained in specificity. (13.4)

My heart longs for the awakening of worlds, for the forthcoming unveiling of the living cosmoi of multiple worlds and stars, for the wide spectrum of all-conscious-life inscribed in the heart, soul, and mind of every living creature. But if we cannot demonstrate our capacity to protect and nurture life here, in this world, by what right may we claim a place among a multitude of other ascended worlds? How can we make our worth known when we trample, ignore, and deny life as it withers in our self-preoccupations, disrespect, and cold indifferences? (13.5)

To know the sacred human is to know the sacredness of all life, to reverence the female, to nurture the children for a hundred generations, to provide shelter for the poor, lost, confused, disoriented, in all forms of life. It is not the human that needs redemption but all life that redeems the human because through maturity and wisdom, humanity finds a task worthy of its deepest potential, to preserve life, to end war, to nurture the garden, the forest, jungle, savannah, oceans, seas and rivers, swamps and meadows, all creatures, to purify and transform. (13.6)

Humanity must curb its expansion, overcome excess and greed, cease tearing down and begin building up by dissolving congestion and over-population in such a rare and gifted world; what does not occur voluntarily will occur involuntarily, what is needed for balance will come, a cloud, a wave, a storm, a terror, depending on the resistance and ignorance that denies all needs but the human. To be sacred in the human is to be sacred through relatedness, extended kinship, and intra-species responsibility. (13.7)

This field of living relations extends into the dream, into mythic worlds, into the vaster Ur-Space of the collective life, into the multidimensional Infinite, where other life-forms await our discovery. It extends into the realms of those that have passed over, disincorporated but alive and active, the afterworlds and other worlds within the psychic, subtle planes, where every species has its Archetypes, its Archons, its primordial images impressed on the fabric of Being, its living emissaries from the Ureal, from the angelic orders, from the hyper-subtle worlds. (13.8)

Many times have I seen the living images, the archetypes and devas, the spirit-being others, the living souls of those no longer corporeal, the animate presence of specific entities, in animate, mystic, surreal forms, alive, active, not projections or mere imaginings, but living ancestral beings seeking to commune. I have been held and entranced, uplifted and spell-bound, mesmerized by the magnitude and diversity. I cannot say I comprehend them, but I hold them as sacred because they hold sentience as dear, life as precious, each being, a gift. (13.9)

Every living form is there, in those subtle realms, imprinted in the energetic mysteries of transcorporeal being, not fleeing shadows, but livid, living, intense, vital over-whelming presences, even of non-human origin, reflecting life forms far removed from this world. This "world" is a platform, grounded gravity-space, bending time to slow it to material forms but the world as it truly IS extends "ten fingers beyond" every idea we hold and every theory we claim that would make us sacred. (13.10)

The immeasurable nature of What Is cannot be reduced to the human image or to human dreams of superiority; we are one among many, unique like every species is unique, accomplished only in so far as we escape our own limited appetites and desires and find our true balance, our rightful inheritance to the garden we create, to a harmony between all species and all life forms. Our task is to create the sacred human; to expand mind, heart, and soul to embrace a loving fellowship with all life, in all worlds. (13.11)

We are not alone; we work in relation to worlds and beings greater than our own accomplishments, the uniting energy of Spirit is ever present, weaving the work of subtle partnership through the willing attitudes and efforts of all who care. If we attend, open the heart, calm the mind, create an intent for loving relations, determine to live ethically, non-violently, peacefully, we can learn, become educated, and grow into the sacredness that calls us; through trust, trust is created, through wisdom, wisdom becomes. (13.12)

Living Nature, Holy Earth (14)

The world is a living being, cosmically created through great spans of time and multidimensional space, but not by energy alone; say, rather, by mind and spirit, infused with love, through the condensation of Mystery into forms. This condensation is a compression that creates, giving birth to life in even the smallest particle spun into being for Being's sake. The initial conditions of mind and soul are found there, where the first smallest spark was born, like a luminous atom in the eye of God. (14.1)

When formlessness takes form, a miracle occurs; the possible becomes actual and the actual comes to life, giving further birth through combination. Combination is a Mystery, like water molecules made of oxygen and hydrogen atoms, structure is created but in unique ways with covalent bonds, bent molecules, lone pair electrons that create opportunities for other bonds and structures. Combination is an open process that invites and repels, reflecting the dynamics of constant creation and dissolution. (14.2)

Creation is a constant process of interaction through shared fields of sentience whose smallest forms create quantum links, entangled across unpredictable space and whose largest forms exceed human imagination. Sentience is a property of Spirit and Being that animates the cosmos through a constant arising of life-forms; becoming, combining, giving structure, dying, transforming, shedding energies and acquiring new attributes, all through the medium of an open horizon of Immeasurable scope and depth. (14.3)

Thus our world is animate at the most fundamental base of energetic forms, from subparticles to vibrant strings, multidimensional in the most minute sense, outside of time, primordial particles of a living cosmic process constantly creating. Molecule by molecule form is built, structures give birth to functions, parts differentiate, organs form, perception develops, and consciousness becomes a living, animate, mobile form alive in a swarming sea of vibrant tides that ebb and flow giving eventual rise to mind, awareness, and species life. (14.4)

The elemental qualities carry this sentience—water, earth, air, and fire, wood and metals, gemstones and herbal plants, elements of the period table, ever expanding to accommodate more differentiated types. The stellar influences carry sentience, of a high and subtle astral kind, reflected light of stars, cosmic background radiance, every possible energy type, wave, particle, or quark. The earth is not defined by a single sentience but by an immeasurable host of interactive sentient influences. (14.5)

Imagine all types of sentience, from within the earth, upon the earth, in the waters, in the air, from mantle to core, from highest atmosphere to deepest ocean bottoms, bombarded all by cosmic radiance, stellar, microwave, thermal, hadronic cascades, electromagnetic pulses, all the wavicles of energetic forms, by sun, moon, planetary influences, by astral bacteria and spores, creating a tremendous stimulus for life, for the formation of the Gaia field, birthing a world of beings who must each find a way to survive, flourish, and propagate. (14.6)

This world overflows with life, it is supersaturated, and in the midst is the human exemplar, the creature who stood upright to see the world, who came out of the jungles of primordial life, millions of years in the making, only to forget the bonds of connection between all species, to turn a blind eye to the death of species, to pollute, abuse, cast garbage into seas, create acid rain, fill the air with the noxious scent of industry, chemical waste, and to store nuclear contaminants as a heritage for future generations. (14.7)

I do not feel hope that what has been so marred can easily be repaired or returned to its pristine sentience; massive populations, overcrowding, shortage, mass farming and an exhausted earth seem to lie in the future. What visions come, show crisis, suffering, and only after great change, a rebirth that fully honors the holiness of earth and all created life. We made the road we give our children to walk; we cannot sustain a way of life that denies the sacred depths of creation and seeks only selfish or immediate or monetary satisfactions. (14.8)

But I do not despair nor deny the inevitable rebirth, whatever suffering must come because of ignorance will pass; the world will awaken when the deep sentience that gives life, mind, heart, and soul is fully honored through intelligent actions, moral conscience, and communal efforts. Even now, the weavings in the Gaia field hold fibers of light that sustain a new consciousness that webs the world; held in the energetic arrays of dedicated minds and hearts, I see a birthing ground for world transformation, now dawning. (14.9)

You light workers and soul-makers, you who carry the burden of transformation must not surrender your burdens or obligation; every worker contributes to the change, every soul carries the capacities for contribution, often in subtle influences where sentience can increase and flow more fully into the outworn channels to create the world anew. Those who bring greater sentience into human awareness will honor nature in all Her diversity, celebrate the inflowing cosmic stream that uplifts us all. (14.10)

We call the earth holy because it carries life, because it is the ground of species, of rich ecologies of body, mind, and soul, each with unique aspects and precious attributes. How very sacred is such an earth, not a sterile, dark planetoid but a world of color, green, blue, earth tones, reflected in a rich palette of spectral hues splashed across the world to awaken joy and reverence, because life thrives in all its differences, does not conform to a single type and revels in profound diversities and multitypes. (14.11)

The Gaia field holds all life in the bounty of Her ever changing forms, breathes life into nature and holds the keys of transformation in the secrets of her inmost processes. The sacred sciences of life, those dedicated to reverent discovery, to the intersection of sentience, consciousness, energy, and matter can bring forth an articulation of those secrets through dedication to life, honoring without abuse every creature, all sentience, through a loving attitude that recognizes Being and Spirit present in all discovery. (14.12)

The PanSolar Logos (15)

Most gracious Light! How your sacred life energies abound, filling the world with dawn and twilight, the ever-flowing double band around the turning globe, ever twilight, ever dawn, the reciprocal twins. Warming the earth, activating life, lighting the world, the plants thrive, the waters warm, the clouds birth rain, and fire is an image that drives away the dark, while lightning links earth and sky, reflecting the magnetic coil, like a living serpent of the Sun. (15:1)

Deep core particles of hydrogen fuse into helium, millions of years for those energies to reach radiant space, illumining all; a surface twelve thousand times larger than Earth, a vaster heliosphere of solar light in spiral waves, a ballerina's skirt, flaring forth, a radiant sacred sphere of particles and fields, a sphere more than one hundred fifty times the distance from Earth to Sun. At the boundary, solar winds meet the interstellar media of other stars, a bow wave forms as we travel round the galactic center. (15:2)

Kyklos Galaxias, Circle of Milk or Milky Way, a living sea of stars in circular form, our galaxy, our Sun Helios one among more than two hundred billion astral lights, shining among hundreds of other visible galaxies, some far larger than our own. Our local group of thirty galaxies, a span of ten million light years across, itself part of the two thousand galaxies of the Virgo Supercluster, one of among millions, astral filaments at bubble boundaries. Holy Father of Lights! How beyond the imaginable is the scope of light through Bythos, the Holy Luminous Deep. (15:3)

Heavenly Sun, Helios-Sol, oracular Apollo, Surya, Turquoise Boy, Amaterasu, great Raa-Harakhte, Hawk of the Boat of a Million Years, Tonatiuh the Fifth Sun, ever-resplendent Gucumatz, giver of the crystal seeds of light; all names of the burning Light that fills and illumines this world. The center of our Heliocosm is a living Star, light-giver, life-giver, fire opal of incredible hues and depth and energies; our noble Sun, whose energies and animate particulate photons manifest the wave-particle harmony. (15:4)

Plato taught the ancient mystery of solar intelligence, the enduring dedicated consistency of its ever-shining awareness, beaming forth to inspire every living creature; now we know our star travels about the galactic center, a single orbit in 28,000 light years, the entire human evolution only a small portion of the arc of a single revolution. Billions of years it burns, and billions more to burn, an enduring source of living Light, witness to the rise of all earth life forms, a unique consciousness based in elemental transformation. (15.5)

Light has long been the luminous sign of visionary life, the illumined soul or mind or heart, an indication of true awakening, subtle aura of the living body, soft image of the sun; our transparency, born of alchemical transformation, is also elemental. We arouse the magnetic polarities, balance the wave and particle, in a body that is material, psychic, spiritual, and transcendental; and the animate soul of this body participates in a living intelligence that images the sun's own life, as a self-aware being. (15.6)

In meditation, I reflect on the PanSolar Logos, a luminous intelligence, pervasive and cosmic in origin, linking all stars into a single network of shared intelligences, differentiated by distinct points of light, unitary by the nature of its essence. We too participate in that Logos, as do all living creatures, where every thought, idea, insight, and visionary perception finds a shared transpersonal ground—beyond body, mind, and soul, yet inseparable from their co-creation, this living intelligence stimulates every thinking feeling creature. (15.7)

In prayer, I call upon the PanSolar Logos to guide and instruct my mind and heart, to teach me the way to interact, to be a good relative, a loving friend, a sensitive husband, a brother, teacher, lover, and rightly guided co-creator. Source of inspiration, August Mystery, ancient wisdom Father, luminous Logos Guide to higher life, All-Light Being, sustainer, compassionate, merciful, forgiving, inspiring, source of clarity that purifies and uplifts, illumines to heal, who offers solace and direction without demand. (15.8)

In ecstasy, I have seen, been immersed, overwhelmed by Thy Light, taken out of myself, saturated beyond memory and returned shaken and in awe, sensed directly the limitless extent of wave upon wave of Infinite Light, an Ocean of Being with no bottom, a center without a boundary, my own consciousness a fragile vessel in the midst of an overflowing tide of luminous intelligence, a living sea, a consciousness that is beyond bliss or personal being, wiping clear the smoky glass of my mind that I might behold the Immeasurable. (15.9)

Whatever that Light may be, it encompasses every living star, every astral-stellar form, every aspect of manifest life as Source and Depth, in which the operations of creative construction are mapped to an ever-expanding universe of knowledge, will, and creative synthesis. I cannot say I comprehend It, but I can bear witness to that Presence, I can bear the mark of immersion, I can carry the blessing forward. Words seem inadequate to the Mystery, PanSolar Logos cannot be easily explained, but it can be known. (15.10)

Imagine an invisible network of panascopic links, between stars and worlds, Indra's Net cast on the ocean of the Infinite, each star and each world a jeweled intersection, unique and lustrous, each gem a fractal image of the whole yet itself composed of fractals representing its own unique qualities. Imagine this network as it encompasses a vast reach in multidimensional space while through it flows intelligence, awareness, a supersaturated density of particle-wave knowledge, carried by starlight to each of us. (15.11)

Metaphors suggest—the composition of the Net dissolves in the ocean of possible forms and functions, becoming One Mind, or One Ground and then One Faith, One Path; this is not the way, the mystery that is named is not the true mystery. Only by casting off images, words, thoughts, desires and hierarchic ideas can we attain the deep surrender where Light becomes a medium that leads beyond itself to the most holy Logos that has no sound or form—only ecstasy and grace, absorption and lucid purity of soul. (15.12)

TheaTheos, Spirit All

Holy Mother, Holy Father
Sacred energies of creation, arising, and decline,
Unity in Yum-Yab embrace!

Bless us in our aspirations, our seeking
after Wisdom Insights,
our capacities for an overflowing Heart
our imperfect striving to overcome what we have
yet to comprehend.

Your blessed union, your ecstasy, your overflowing Joy
radiates into the vast Beyond and penetrates
to the Immediacy of the Now;
We behold your Unity as an awe inducing sign
Thea-Theos, Goddess-God, Ament-Ra,
Mother-Earth-Father-Sun
perfectly united and perfectly separable
Illumined Lotus, Rose of Passion.

Planetary Song of Heaven,
sound the Paean of our mutual joy
that we, in Hieros Gamos, may also ascend
to Eros Unity as interpenetrated souls,
to the Far Horizon of brilliant Ra,
to the dark Earth Bed of Phusia, to the swollen belly
of life's becoming, to the birthing ground
of new life born to attain harmonic joy, a perfect fifth,
a unison of concord and discovery.

May Spirit bless our praxis, our aspiration,
our attempted versions to surpass
all imitation, to be life-source,

to attain to a resonance that reflects
the energies of a unitary cosmos,
to bless our synthesis,
to make Love a burning ember
a Fire whose heat
Endures.

May TheaTheos grant us Visions,
make us paramours of Wisdom
gift us with intelligence for the doing
of Good, grant us Compassion
for All shared Becoming.

Blessed is the Light of that Union, so far
Beyond our own self striving
so Great in Overcoming,
so Vast in Being
Beyond Self, yet
utterly All.

TheaTheos, guide us on our Paths!

Lux Sophiana (16)

This Wisdom is subtle, not simply dense with abstraction, not erudite, but heart-centered, feeling the world as a living, layered process of self-discoveries. This is Wisdom arising through interaction, where solitude and self-reflection are images of refined and remembered encounters: in visions, dreams, mystical moments, in a book, a conversation, or a sudden intuition carried in psychic currents created through a soulful, shared world. (16.1)

As dawning Light, subtle, soft, and vibrant, in intuitive flashes, momentary insights, sudden realizations, this Wisdom is our guide, teacher, companion. Like a spark, a burning ember, a heartfelt concern that urges change or challenges resistant ways of thought or action, Lux Sophiana is an infelt sense of correctness, appropriate response, a path that leads to moral conscience, right behavior, and trustworthy relations. This is the light of soul come forth, urging authenticity. (16.2)

Such authenticity balances the masculine and the feminine, understands the *Hieros Gamos*, the sacred marriage, gained through social harmony and cooperative partnership, through inner reflections and positive growth in relationships. Wisdom Light reveals the hard lessons of encounter soften by acknowledging limits and the overcoming of poor habits, self-serving attitudes, and blindness instilled by conformity to inflexible codes of imbalance and limited hierarchy. (16.3)

Gender balance is a spiritual necessity, not a cultural attitude, a deep and profound right for each being, a path to the full realization of human potential mediated by unique talents, individual commitments, and dedication to cooperative ideals. Wisdom seeks partnership, flourishes through love and respect, and comes into the brilliance of its promise alight with joy because that Wisdom is shared, flowing across boundaries, opening eyes and minds and hearts, giving and receiving. (16.4)

Wisdom is cocreated, born in the light of mindfulness, animated by love, mutual concerns, and dedicated mutuality. It is seen in the eyes of children who have no fear, lucid like animal intelligence, as a deep curiosity about the world, others, the strange, the beautiful, the ultradimensional glimmers that penetrate the mundane world and fill it with wonder, fascination, and sacred encounters. Not mundane wisdom, but spiritual Wisdom illumining mind. (16.5)

Such Wisdom is subtle, soft, feminine, born out of faithful observation and gracious attitudes of mind harmonious with Unseen Reality; it is a form of spontaneity whose contents vary according to the needs of each individual mediated by larger needs shared across multiple communities. It is a Wisdom that skips, like subtle lightening, linking viable worlds, heaven above and earth below, in sudden insights illuminating a dark corner with new possibilities. (16.6)

It is a prayerful Wisdom, we can reach it inwardly through dedicated aspirations but I cannot determine its outflow nor its consequence; like a dove sent flying into a clear sky, I cannot tell where it might land, but I do know it will return, bringing a gift, an olive branch, a rose, a thorn, a flash of conscience, a determination to overcome old patterns for new made ways. Wisdom prayer is not an asking as much as a receiving, a gift that comes veiled and must be carefully unwrapped to preserve its unique qualities. (16.7)

There is a blessing in this Wisdom, this Light, this Lux Sophiana—a sense of living Presence that soothes and heals and gives new life; like the transparent blue of Mary's robe, like the golden roses at her feet, like the diadem on her brow, there is a blessing that permeates, shines forth, instills gratitude, awe, and reverence and yet, asks for nothing, demands nothing, gives freely without expectation in order to make a clear path for self-determined action, to ignite a living heart. (16.8)

Opening to this Wisdom requires an open mind, a mind free of preoccupations, expectations, demands or needs that obscure and cloud the possible Light. Gratitude is primary, receptivity to what may be rather than what is, a willingness to listen, great patience, inner calm, a genuine commitment to return, again and again, to that state of openness to the Infinite, because it is there, in the Infinite, that Wisdom arises, takes form, and distills a consequence into a finite heart. (16.9)

They say that Yeshu'a as a child, took a clay bird in his hand, breathed upon it, and the clay bird became a living bird, then flew away. This is a Wisdom teaching, the clay bird is a mind held captive to material reality, the breath is the living Spirit infusing life into dead matter, and the hand is the soul that gives life, no longer limited to material thought. The parable teaches that innocence, as in a child, can bring new life through the wonder that Wisdom gives from the very moment of our conception. (16.10)

The bird that takes wing is a living sign, a *synthemata*,

manifesting a miracle, a token expression of the Hidden Reality, a *symbolicon*, a lively image of mind revealing latent capacity, to give life, awareness, intelligence, through the gift of healing, transmutation, an infusion that makes real, turning material into spiritual, into Mystery. It is Wisdom to see into these parables, to imagine the possible in the visible form, to celebrate the latent through an actualization that is free to take its own flight. (16.11)

The Lux Sophiana is an inexhaustible resource for all forms of spiritual awaking, in all traditions, taking on the unique contents, or contentlessness, of what is sought in the hearts and souls of each living creature; tradition, transtraditional, non-traditional, spontaneously adapted by context and capacity, this Wisdom sparks realizations, a science of soul whose depths cannot be measured, challenging us to abandon doubt and embrace the overflowing fullness. (16.12)

Dreams, Visions, Ecstasies (17)

The histories of religious traditions are replete with visionaries, mystics, seers and sages whose spiritual encounters, realizations, or revelations come through the media of Spirit infused into mind; not through reason or logic, but through visionary constructions, future becoming is made transparent. The visionary capacity is the natural child of mind and Spirit conjoined, where Spirit gives depth and fullness and mind shapes meaning into interpretation. (17.1)

Living Spirit, Holy Mother Light, holds the soul in stasis, uplifted to a seeing that is beyond mind, and mind becomes the media for the synthesis of visionary contents made accessible to the minds and hearts of others. What is seen, heard, felt in that altered visionary state cannot be adequately described in words, in arbitrary signs, or fixated images. It is a living medium of dynamic encounter revealing cosmic depths. (17.2)

The dream has many forms, and no one form expresses the actual nature of the dreaming, no one content or manifest dream can fully represent the dreaming capacity; our dreaming abilities range across a wide spectrum of states and some states enter into the mystical domain, revealing through transparency, lucid capacities of soul. This higher dreaming is a form of *gnosis*, a true immersion in ecstatic insights, revealing new modes of cognition, transforming awareness into new knowledge. (17.3)

The Aeons of dreaming are Hermetic signs of awakening, archetypes of encounter, angels of insight, Holy Spirituals that manifest a sacred content and act to illumine a mind suspended in sleep, yet open to encounters that can shock the soul out of its complacency, challenging us to reconstruct the mundane world into a more vivid spiritual domain, imbued with spiritual presence, entities, healing agents of change. (17.4)

The Hermetic dream, the gnostic encounter, the visionary impact of the sacred Other is a path into the Infinite mediated by specific capacities and talents. All dreamers may have these dreams, but only some dreamers can remember and bring to mind the conscious imprint of encounter, can interpret the meaning, can bring into view the value and worth that weaves meaning into the context and makes the dream a guide. (17.5)

Great dreams are not the only way, even small dreams, dreams of everyday, dreams that seem of less account can be made meaningful through insights arising out of reflection on their contents; dreaming is a medium of contact, a revelatory ground whose metacosmic dimensions can reach into vastness and yet, instill insights into the everyday—a dream is a possibility, any dream can be a sign to the observant dreamer. (17.6)

The art of dream interpretation is ancient; humanity has always dreamed, always been informed by dream figures, archetypal encounters, visionary angelic forms manifesting new intelligence concerning human destiny and possible pathways. The dream is enigmatic, socially unbound, surreal, liminal, at times dark and shadowy, arising from the human psyche not yet subtle as the soul of its origins. (17.7)

For many years, from childhood to old age, dreams have guided my path, shown me both the metacosmic beyond and the dangers of missteps that only imitate authenticity, revealing noble and less noble actions, challenging my beliefs or attitudes of mind. The dream brings me back to soul, to the unknown country of possibilities, to the as yet unrealized embodiment of soulful being, not yet fully actualized. The dream is oracular, a potential requiring reflection. (17.8)

We are each a dream in process, each manifesting an inner reality of becoming through select actions and beliefs, infused with collective mental attitudes, imbued with the ethos of correct becoming, at times misled or confused, some dangerously aggressive about the dream they hold as a necessary truth. Dreams of cooperation, world peace, gender equality, species respect and a non-violent spirituality are Hermetic dreams—they foster alchemical change for the Good, they teach us shared pathways. (17.9)

What is ecstasy? It is a capacity to be taken out of one's ordinary state, lifted above daily concerns and worries, transfigured through encounters that open a vaster horizon of awareness in the context of infused insight. The ecstatic dream is a path of transformation, of revelatory states and profound depths, that takes each dreamer beyond the margins of normalcy and into the mythic, the sacred, the holy Deep. (17.10)

Not all dreams come in sleep, some come while awake, fully conscious, as visionary realizations, transparently opening into a cosmic web of psychic and soulful relations; these waking dreams, these manifestations of the Imaginal, are vivid presentments whose Holy Spiritual nature requires our utmost efforts to understand. Nothing is as it seems, nothing is simply literal, everything is metamorphic, subject to interpretation, each dream a multiperspective. (17.11)

The dream, the vision, a waking sacred encounter is an inexhaustible resource for the comprehension of the human and transhuman, a window on soul's life, a medium for encounter with the dead, the angelic, the demonic, the surreal and unknown. We all dream and whoever does not attend to their dreams, sleeping or waking, does not know the soul's depths; the Hermetic path celebrates the dream and seeks to integrate it as a primary source of insights, revelation, and contact with the Most Holy. (17.12)

Ur-Space and the Heliocosm (18)

How Vast it is! This hypercosm, this Infinite heaven filled with megaforms in dancing motion, expanding and contracting, dying and giving birth, filled with energetic waves, particles, fields, conjunctions and ionic repulsions; a vast network of stellar influences infused with Spirit mediated through every manifestation great or small. A living cosmos! An immeasurable context whose dimensions, domains, branes or superstrings, provide a dynamic context for life in many forms, from material to immaterial, from visible to invisible, from conscious to superconscious. (18.1)

We do not know the fullness of this cosmic Reality, only its forms and surfaces as we gaze outwardly, astonished by complexity, motion, interaction, creation or recreation. And every star a possible home of conscious life, layered from gross to subtle, from minute awareness to more comprehensive knowing, each star a Heliocosm, a local system, our Sun's planets, moons, astral bodies, comets, particulate matter-energies surging throughout the Whole. (18.2)

Gazing inwardly, we discover Ur-Space, a primordial context supporting Imaginal and Visionary capacities, the dream-spaces of out-of-body travel, near-death encounter, astral projection and openness to angelic interactions; this is mind-space, soul-space, consciousness extended beyond body into multidimensional domains where psychic principles manifest through interaction and relationships with subtle Others. (18.3)

This primordial Ur-space encompasses all that is outer with all that is inner, inseparable from the Heliocosm, it infuses our stellar system from the heart of Sun to the heliopause where solar winds meet the interstellar matrix, bringing Imaginal life to all aspects, knowable through visionary encounter. Once called World-Soul, *Anima Mundi*, it is a Hermetic Heliocosm, a Sun whose light gives life and irradiates a psychic vastness barely comprehensible. (18.4)

Ur-Space is enfolded space, concealed in the space-time matrix as an inner dimension whose contents incorporate and coordinate inner and outer, where a dreamer may travel to other worlds, to the realms of the post-mortem, to subtle domains infusing Phusia, Holy Nature feminized, as the Mother Ground for all animate life in whatever form or kind. This inner Hermetic journey crosses a *herm*, a boundary, collapses inner and outer into a seamless, complex multispace in which worlds take form and variegate beings inhabit an interactive cosmos. (18.5)

We are each a participant in this matrix of Ur-Space, interconnected through mind and soul, though *psyche* and *nous*, with both the very ground of Being and the interactive multispectral fields of Becoming. There is a great Continuum, a transcosmic domain of communication between and across worlds, star to star, sun to sun, being to being, World-Soul to World-Soul, linked through the innate communicative potential of Ur-Space. (18.6)

I have entered that domain, been awakened to its call, heard its urgent desire for communication linking worlds and beings whose minds and souls are receptive to the Great Work, the uplift of a world, an awakening of the entire Heliocosm to its stellar fellowship among the living heavens wide with waking dreamers, rich with information, overflowing with connectedness beyond description, utterly animate with billions of life forms. (18.7)

Such knowledge is difficult to sustain, a rare event in my limited capacity, therefore it flashes forth dense with intensity meant to support climatic realizations on a global scale, a transhistorical opening whose forms and actualizations depend upon a wide array of circumstances and beings supporting inner growth and transformation. Many are called to this work, to embody a new mind open to a soulful cosmos, that an entire world may awaken to its inheritance and membership in transcosmic, mutual co-participation. (18.8)

Such realization is the work of many generations of change, growth, development, regressions overcome for new insights motivating decisive action. Those who bear this promise, revealed in turbulent dreams and visions, in poetic metaphor and imaginative discourse, in philosophy and science, in innumerable areas of human work and creative exploration, are the mediums through which this change can fully Actualize. (18.9)

There is a chaotic aspect, a turbulence in becoming that seeks to absorb the past in the face of a changing present, open to future transformations. This chaos is creative but also in overturning old ways, it leaves uncertainty and often confusion it its wake, in those still clinging to old ways and forms. We can hold to the past, value what was, but the processes of Becoming require a new stability able to shed old skin and reveal new patterns meant to assimilate chaos into a novel forms of future realization. (18.10)

No one person represents this change, no individual embodies the fullness of this Becoming and all contribute to the realization or retardation of its promise; Ur-Space is the arena of exploration, the multidimensional context of psychic life liberated from strict materialism and contracted doubts; also active in Ur-space are counter notes against an over romantic theme of inevitability—it is not inevitable, but possible; it may, not will, occur. (18.11)

Regardless of the consequence, the Heliocosm beams forth its life signature across stellar distances and throughout inner space; it stimulates growth and desire, broadcasts the spectrum of a life inhabiting world whose many beings, visible and invisible, contribute to an arising possibility to attain to higher realizations, a *gnosis*, mapped to cosmic trans-stellar co-existence through the mediums of Ur-space where multiple worlds and beings await our discovery. (18.12)

All Above and All Below

An Endless Sea of All-Seeing,
Being Unveiled, as a partial tributary
flowing forth from Ocean, cannot reveal
the Magnitude or Mystery of
the Unimaginable.

Holy Mother, Father Light!
May daughters and sons of humanity seek
the pathways of inspiration leading to
new realizations in Spirit, in Fire inspired by
the opening of the Holy Lotus
of the Heart.

May our children inherit a worthy world of peace,
overcoming our violent tendencies of the past,
leading exemplary lives of caring
for the health of others, for the safety of all,
in support of every creature, creating a
loving world of mutual, shared
well-being.

All above and all below shall be our song,
we will sing the chorus of mutual
consent to be bringers of Light,
givers of goodness, healers, teachers,
visionaries guided by Inner Clarity
dedicated to Thee, the Unnamable Source
Beyond Father or Mother
Sons and Daughters All Spirit Born
on wings uplifted by Grace
to fully Know, to Love, and
to receive with gratitude

Your gifts in a Cosmos
most mysterious and vast.

We give thanks, we reverence the
gift of life, our beloved partners, our
relations with all those we know,
we celebrate our gifts and all the gifts
of Others, in peace we know them
and in peace we are known by them.

May Spirit hear our prayers
and may our words reach
receptive hearts, may
our souls aligned.
Shanti!

The God Light Within (19)

The God Light is Spirit Presence within all beings, within a cosmos and a particle of sand; it is the living Source of contact with the Most Holy, a glowing ember, a spark, a magical touch, a felt sense of the Great More, a testimony of awakening, overcoming the unfelt soul for new life, rebirth and reconstitution in the form of unique and powerful inspirations, or as a simple, gentle, delicate touch, like a breeze carrying a lotus scent. (19.1)

This Light is sacred, an immaterial illumination taking the form of visible light but more profound, Spirit opening mind to soul and soul to the Infinite, not in darkness or in a void, but in abundant Fullness, an immeasurable *Pleroma* of God-filled Presence. Present in All, this Light illumines and contains All; the distinction between the "inner and outer" diminishes as we enter into co-participation, infused within and without by that Light, Unity over-spilling. (19.2)

This is Light inseparable from mind and soul, even body is infused with this Light variated according to structure, form, and function—the heart-light, the body auras, the electromagnetic currents of psycho-neural interactions, radiation signatures, magnetic fields, and other yet-to-be discovered properties all co-participate in this Light. Such Light is complex not simple, supersaturated with energy, mind, and Spirit, a treasure trove of implicate possibilities. (19.3)

Such Light is knowable, the root source of Hermetic Illumination, an indwelling, upswelling, undying reminder of latent capacities evolving through incarnate processes to refine, develop, and multiply unrealized potentials. We cannot fathom it because it has no measure, no dimensional attributes, no instantiation but the Whole, the All That Is, the full process dynamics of All Becoming; knowable through *gnosis* but beyond measure, seen, but not fully comprehended. (19.4)

Source of mind and soul, this Light is animate, inextricably conscious, inevitably superconscious, ultimately beyond consciousness, merging into depths and fullness where words exhaust their meanings and mind becomes enstatic, a phenomenal sign, a *sunthēmata*, manifest as a vast, limitless expanse of utterly luminous Being and Becoming. Mind can enter into that ecstasy, but it does not become thus all-knowing, only more knowing of the Unknowable. (19.5)

This Light is oracular, it instills inspiration and uplifts understanding in the human context, prehending mind and pointing it toward future possibility, toward an as yet unrealized outcome without explanation or rationalizing; a vivid presentment coded in visible signs and actions but animated by an inner clarity that is self-surpassing and self-directing. The oracular ramifications are vaster than ordinary knowing, extending into qualities of mind and soul that required utmost attention, stillness, and a deep inner silence. (19.6)

The God Light Within is ever present, ever active, ever life giving and ever subtle, infusing incarnate life with possible direction, urging clarity of intent, a more purposeful commitment to life values that sustain that very inspiration as shared and interactive across a multitude of hearts and minds. Specially known, it is ordinarily present, illuming minds, it is an inextinguishable Cause, a stimulus toward greater maturity, a deep insight, a more compassionate heart, a more dedicated way of life. (19.7)

I have known that Light, been overwhelmed by its magnitude and uplifted by a scale of vastness I cannot comprehend; the God Light Without is a boundless Sea of Awareness, where the "I" becomes a fragile glass filled to overflowing Fullness and thus, carried beyond taste or touch or sense, each remembered in distant, weaker reflections. The God Light Within is an enduring presence, a gentle touch, a grace promising illumined sensory awareness; they merge these two, Within and Without, forming Lux Sophiana, Higher Wisdom Unveiled. (19.8)

Inevitably, we ask if this merging, this great Continuum, instills a specific content, a lesson or laws of nature and becoming; I have not found it so. No, this Light is a revelation of What Is, not what might become or how it may grasped; more a depth immersion whose outcomes, oracular in nature, are left to the responsible soul to express in limited conceptions, poetic phrases, and metaphoric imagery, formative impressions whose words and contents reflect the soul, not the undefinable Light. (19.9)

All words reflect this Light, even words of hate and fear, because all life depend upon that Light for its survival and continuation. Most words are contractions, broken signs crushed by repetition and abuse, flung out without real meaning, spoken and recycled endlessly through ingrained habit, poor elementals, habituated awareness, traditionalized social circumstances, but not dead, still carrying inner signs of life because that life lives in and through Spirit; thus, words make Light visible if well-spoken, loving, conscious, grateful, and inspired. (19.10)

More than words, it is actions and thoughts that matter; it is intentions held deep and brought to a focal point that seeks spiritual affirmation and guidance, not a weak desire, but a powerful, dedicated, passionate search for this Light. This is a path, a way, a journey of soul whose determination must be strong enough to overcome skepticism, doubt, boredom, self-indulgence, indifference, fear, and lazy habits of body and mind. This Light is born is the passionate heart of a true spiritual seeker, calling unexpectedly through dreams and intuitions. (19.11)

Seekers of soulful life must aspire, not abandon the quest, must climb the barren hills, seeking the Waters of Life to be revived, find in their dark night, a welcome flash of inspiration pointing the way forward. The God Light Within is always there, awaiting acknowledgement, not demanding, but patient, alert, ever-ready to flare forth in a burst of sudden insight, or to seep into awareness, pressing us toward new insight, sometimes gentle, sometimes through grief, sometimes unexpected and without precedence. (19.12)

Holy Communion of Souls (20)

We are all in communion at a deep soul level, not consciously and not by intent, but spontaneously through birth and death, through the on-going cycles of nature, through the luminous processes of cosmos and becoming. Our souls are not limited by body processes but extend beyond the immediacy of body being receptive to the energies, thoughts, feelings, and imagery of others; our family, friends, relatives, community, work place and play place, through the ever-active interchange of the Ever Now present through hyperconscious connections. (20.1)

The spiritual path is communal, not through joining or conscious membership, but through Spirit as the medium of our shared concerns. There is a vast Continuum through which psychic life washes onto the shores of our waking and sleeping lives, bringing with it, the subtle and at time shocking imagery of other lives, other beings, other entities, also alive and conscious. We share in the Continuum, casting our thoughts, feelings, and imagery across far boundaries, as a shared tide that ebbs and flows, a single thought carries far beyond the thinker. (20.2)

This ebb and flow includes the far past and future as part of the Ever Now present, such that the mind of a focal soul can extend influence in a widening gyre, an expanding circle of creative thought pushing through the dense material of lesser awareness to offer a sacred moment of insight. Great works, inspired texts, sacred scriptures, a poem, a science formula can all transmit, transgress the limits of its birth moment to create a wavicle of influence refracted across the matrix of shared interests even subconsciously received. (20.3)

This communion is "holy" not because of its content but through the medium of its transmission, the sacred ground through which all thought and feeling flows, the pansentient cosmos of unending communication whose energies provide the context for shared awareness. Not propagated through "space" but mind to mind, heart to heart, soul to soul, a non-local transmission not dependent upon spatial propagation but instantly received, point to point, a sudden inflow stimulated by a far-reaching mind elsewhere in a cosmological medium able to know, transmit, and to receive. (20.4)

A molecule of thought finds resonance with other molecules, a shared sensitivity for a single spark of insight; the communion of souls is not based in beliefs or faith, but transmits through the pervasive medium of Abundant Presence, regardless of belief or disbelief. Presence is an intelligible medium that permeates to the core, every molecule of thought, enlivened by a superabundant, indwelling dynamic not confined by form or structure, surpassing every boundary and extending "ten fingers beyond". (20.5)

Souls commune in many ways, not just through thought or feeling, but also through lived experience that creates shared refractions of collective events; every event sends a ripple and every ripple reflects into other ripples, creating multiple accords and unexpected discords, assonance and dissonance, transmogrifying into yet new variants like sudden star bursts, a vast firework of brilliant color, form and yet, dissolving, momentary energies, constantly renewed and then, absorbed. (20.6)

Soul communion occurs through a shared sense of wonder, a capacity for joy and amazement, for sorrow and suffering, hope and regret, for shared memories and dreams. Communion flows through shared experiences, the ground of our interactions magnified in dramas of species evolution, our collective struggles, wars, cultural fluorescence, economic, political and religious developments, inevitable decline, staged in cycles, marked by millennial changes, some invisible and yet, additive to the whole. (20.7)

I have felt communion with others, telepathic, psychic, empathic, in the present, in the past, even the far future, a soul sharing sometime from distant worlds and beings far removed from local space and time. This communion was effortless, a natural link formed by shared developmental moments of awakening to the larger concourses of mind and soul within a living cosmos of beings able to escape local immediacy for far-reaching soul-to-soul contacts in a context of momentary illumination. (20.8)

Our shared soul discoveries are not isolated moments, even when seen and known by only one individual. Such seeing is a medium of transmission in which contents transmute into subtle forms as an indwelling point of awareness harmonic with other similar points, in other minds, creating shared, inner frequencies, subtle patterns concurrent within multiple centers. Communion is a matter of discovery, an awakening to ideas, images, other beings, whose state is receptive to such awakenings. (20.9)

This sharing of insights is a soul aspect of Being, a vibrant compound of integrity and self-awareness mixed with a sympathetic sense of others as partners in the processes of discovery. It is "soulful" because the insights and realizations, are transparent, like deep ocean creatures, sea angels, whose water is the all-embracing source of their life, whose media are multiple currents that nurture intelligence, alive with the electric glow of discovery, radiant in the deep, transmitting shared realizations. (20.10)

Our soul is not bound by body limits; it is a process entity based in forms beyond the protoplasmic, a transtemporal, transpatial being whose memories, thoughts, and degree of awareness reflect a long, multi-life existence capable of transiting between physical, psychic, and transpersonal perspectives, between multiple domains, between immersive and expansive states. In those expansive moments, we become aware of our bonds with others, our psychic attachments and proclivities, our spiritual unity. (20.11)

Co-creation is a spiritual norm, a *nomos* of the spheres, not didactic or demanding but subtle, provocative, compelling as in love and concern for the well-being of others; we work together even while apart, pursue worthy goals even if defined differently. It is not a collective necessity but a shared opportunity, a confirmation of the relevance of every soul in contributing to the Whole; however far removed from community, each of us matter, every thought and action, a possible contribution. (20.12)

Avatars, Saints, and Guides (21)

There are many teachers, guides and thought leaders, all offering perspectives and insights in accord with their understanding. Every teacher can be a guide and every student can learn to teach; there is reciprocity in the learning process that is cyclical, every participant contributing to the expansiveness of that cycle. Learning is a process of constant reconstruction—we learn, unlearn, relearn—building our knowledge base through all our relationships, not simply internal, but shared. (21:1)

A guide helps you to unlearn what inhibits growth and development, but also, a guide challenges you to think beyond the boundaries of your ordinary beliefs and thoughts. A guide can push you toward a realization but then, you must decide on the value and worth of that realization. Realization is not the goal, it is a stage that requires assessment, critical reflection, and assimilation of the outcomes most worthy of your most mature ideals, of the fit between what Is and what can Be. (21.2)

A guide is a helper and model whose authority is relative to your needs, to the assessment of those needs; inquiry is part of the process of discovery, reflection must not simply mirror the world but also shine light into the deepest shadows. There is also inner guidance, a sense of direction based on insights arising from that same depth; such guidance has many forms, dreams, intuitions, visions or spontaneous, participatory moments—filled with light, illumination, and sometime shadows. (21.3)

No guide is perfect is all ways, every guide has his or her limitations, boundaries acquired over a lifetime of learning; the best guides are those who do not celebrate their wisdom, who can be utterly down-to-earth, normal, but not superficial or lacking the subtle presence of true knowing. Perfection is not the goal, imperfection is a shallow sandbar covered by an ocean of possibility; we can wash away both perfection and imperfection for a deeper, freer, less complex existence. (21.4)

What is a saint? A person who becomes an ideal expression of an existential condition, one who illumines a field greater than personal or individual awareness; it is a person of great integrity whose path culminates in direct knowing, circumstantially conditioned by tradition, place, time, and cultural context. Such a person offers radiance, sending subtle influences that are psychically powerful and profound. (21.5)

A saint, as Christian, Muslim, Hindu, Sikh or a Bodhisattva of Buddhist orientation, a Daoist master, or Master Shaman, all contribute to our understanding of the possible made visible through direct knowing. In prayer, contemplation, meditation, ritual action, ceremony, trance and dance, or a multitude of inner techniques, states and insights are acquired and transmitted, often spontaneously, to impact those less aware with a taste of the Infinite hidden in the mundane. (21.6)

Every saint has qualities, not just attributes, but living qualities of the Sacred Ground, immanent within the material body and radiant through the subtle, intelligible, emotional, psychic, and spiritual aspects of individual embodiment. Each is different, each realization a unique accomplishment, a creative concatenation whose embodiment is engendered by a much deeper Ground, an ever-prompting Presence, whose depths support an unlimited possibility of types and kinds. (21.7)

I have met such persons, in dreams, visions, and waking, very vivid and alive with Spirit, lucid and communicative, sharing insights, giving initiations, transmitting knowledge often well beyond my comprehension, at times revealing domains and dimensions of Reality far beyond my ken, an invitation to reach out, extend, open to the unknown. But there is simplicity there as well, directness and luminosity that washes away all limitation and doubt, a knowing transmitted silently, gratefully received. (21.8)

There are also those called Avatars, direct manifestations of Godly nature whose existence challenges all material theory and whose luminosity overshadows any evolutionary theory. Full and complete they say, without previous lifetimes, a unique Being, God-saturated, Luminous, Ever-Shining, an archetype of archetypes, an Aeon directly manifest from Godhood. I respectfully acknowledge such Beings, without knowing or comprehending their actual Beingness, a sacred Mystery. (21.9)

There have been many actual Avatar manifestations in many different cultures, even in Native American traditions, and especially in India, land of Avatars! And these august Beings continue to appear, even in my own lifetime, I met at least one, Sri Ma, whose voice was profoundly uplifting and whose music lifted my soul to a far horizon beyond everyday seeing. Incarnational presence is communicated in subtle form, like music, a harmonic frequency filled with life and joy. (21.10)

There is a similarity between Avatar and Holy Spiritual, each is an *Ishtadeva*, a God-form—and when the body dies, the Avatar may become reabsorbed into Mystery, or perhaps becomes a Holy Spiritual, a divine form no longer physical, but accessible through dreams and visions. The Holy Mother Spirit has many forms, Her eyes a penetrating crystal blue, Her glance like a shockwave, overturning expectations and revealing hidden depths yet to learn. (21.11)

Teachers, guides, masters, saints, Avatars all can assist us in our journey, but in the end, it is soul and mind that must do the work, make the right decisions and act in accord with the highest ideals—not the teacher and not the student, but the soulful individual striving to self-surpass; soul-striving and soul-arriving require utmost dedication and then, a willingness to let-go, release, suspend judgment in order to attain the proper mind and heart awareness, ever-learning soul-surrender. (21.12)

Metacosmic Sympathies

We all suffer!
We long for inner wisdom but
act without discretion, forgiving ourselves
because we lack the understanding to
better serve our mutual needs.

Holy Mother!
Where is wisdom in the face of Chaos?
How can an impoverished people
gain the necessary insight
to endure a transformation
that takes us beyond our selfish needs,
that opens a doorway into a
vaster cosmology,
a more luminous heaven?

We seek Wisdom
without understanding the need for
self-surpassing, and the mass collective
roils with turmoil,
surges against itself,
is flooded by tides of resistance
armored in lies and self-delusions,
lost, thinking itself found,
fearful but lashing out,
regretful but full of pride!

Holy Mother show us nurture
and guide us on a path of
reconciliation, new hope,
bounty based in shared
concerns, love freely

given, respecting
every person.

Love is not a banner or flag to wave
but an interior state, a blessing,
a feeling of connection made
through Holy Ground,
Thy Presence as an
enduring gift,
a touch, a kiss
with no demand,
a subtle joy that links
two souls in a widening arc of
love, that in the end, encompasses
the entire World and all other lovers!

Bless us and show us the Way!

The Suffering of Beings (22)

Suffering is part of life, but it is not the consequence of embodiment, nor the result of incarnation. The causes of suffering are many but in the most direct sense, suffering is the result of decisions and lack of decisions; choices we made or unmade with consequences and these consequences are years and many lives in the making. Suffering is a trial, a tribulation, a difficulty that requires self-assessment, and sometimes, assistance. (22.1)

Some suffering is collective, a storm, a fire, a sweeping illness, an upheaval, a revolt, unjust persecutions, or bias that results in harm and injury; attitudes that create suffering are passed generation to generation out of ignorance, pride, and self-inflated assumptions based often on racial, sexual, social or economic discrimination. Suffering is caused by ignorance and indifference, tragedy and unpredictable chaotic events washing over individuals like a tsunami of unexpected force threatening old foundations. (22.2)

We can distinguish between acts of nature and human acts of predation, war, hatred, and prejudice; between cosmological events impacting a majority, a flood or an earthquake, and personal suffering as a result of unexpected violence, social unrest, illness, or irresponsible, self-centered behaviors whose impact increases suffering, not just for one but for many. Human suffering is an unexpected outcome, conditioned by chaotic influences and often shaped by rigid attitudes and harmful values. (22.3)

Human life is turbulent, capable of great disorder and mental-emotive confusion, rooted in narrow views and biased attitudes; psychically we can attract negative outcomes, resist change to embrace old habits, reinforce ignorance and mistreatment. These negative outcomes reflect choices we make, even in the midst of chaotic events, we can make better choices, less likely to produce suffering. Suffering is not escapable but its consequences can be moderated and lead at times to new insights. (22.4)

Suffering can be a teacher, a difficult path that requires deconstruction of naive views, a confrontation with one's own limits, with resistance based on what is already lost, a beloved partner deceased or divorced, a child lost, a parent now dead, an animal companion now gone. Loss can lead to suffering as a natural outcome of our attachment to love and passion, engagement with others part of our lives, to the fullness that another can add, or to challenges from others necessary for our own growth. (22.5)

But suffering does not define life or incarnation. I characterize life as joyful, creative, sympathetic, and challenging while suffering is a scarlet thread woven into the fabric of the everyday, a vein whose lifeforce is part of the processes of discovery and growth, when cut, that life blood flows forth staining the lived present and endangering our health and well-being. But we can heal, recover, heal the wound and while we carry the scars, we can also continue the journey, keep learning, growing. (22.6)

If we live in shadows, in the dark corners of abased life, clinging to destructive habits and imagining that such a way of life is part of the predatory cycles of rulers and servants, bosses and henchmen, then we become the agents of suffering, servants to a harmful self-serving view whose gratitude is only found by enslavement, obedience, and the constant threat of punishment. The old gods were like that, full of threats, violence, and opulent rewards for servitude. (22.7)

I resisted the old gods and when I turned away, looking east toward the great Asian traditions, I found life characterized as suffering (and illusions) based on false desires, requiring a monastic cure, a dedicated life apart from the world. But that was not life as I found it, I suffered in various ways, but by no means did it defined my whole being as an incarnate soul; instead, I felt the joy and power of life ever-overflowing, carrying me beyond suffering into the beauty of world creation. (22.8)

There is deep chaotic suffering, whole civilizations can suffer through invasion, colonial dominance, religious aggression, or out-and-out war. Such suffering is driven by human motives based in an ethos of dominance and control, aggrandizement meant to form a repressive ideology requiring absolute submission, both suffer, the predator and the victim, but the victim carries the weight of the oppression, not just in this life but in future lives as well. (22.9)

The predator thinks dominance is its own reward, blind to the deep effects of action on the perpetrator; consequential effects reverberate into the transtemporal domains, shaping future outcomes, where predator becomes victim in a confusing swirl of counter-motives and cross-currents breaking the symmetry of well-planned oppressions. Probability as a stochastic matrix shapes future consequences in ways unimaginable to the enclosed, narrow horizon of our current self-knowing. (22.10)

Life is not suffering, but suffering is a consequence of ignorance, or denial, an outcome of rejection of the anomalous and the unseen potential for change and growth; we suffer because we cannot find the proper solution, which is not rejection of the world or escape into some higher transcendence. No, the way forward is through incarnation, through the cultivation of wisdom, maturity, insight, and creative relationships that maximize shared joy and embodied harmony with others. (22.11).

Suffering is a torch, a light that shows our fallibilities, a flare that threatens stability and contentment, but it is also a guide to where the work must be done, where efforts and intentions must be developed in order to overcome suffering, in order to find a new center of being, a shared realization that suffering is the very context that must be healed for all beings, not just to relieve personal stress and strain, but a reconstitution of our deep potential for peaceful, cooperative, creative life together. (22.12)

Madness and Mystery (23)

What is sanity? What is madness? How does one support the other? Sanity reflects inherited social norms, customs, and attitudes of obedience to shared collective expectations. But sanity can oppress, norms can dominate, and obedience may conform to extremes enforced by violence and punishment. Women understand, they have suffered long, hard oppressions; children too have suffered, beaten and battered by sane adults. Madness can be caused by sanity that refuses to adapt or show compassion. (23.1)

Madness is a stage, a liminal interval between states of greater and lesser conformity. Sometimes madness is long enduring, sometimes brief, sometimes sporadic and unpredictable, sometimes withdrawn and at other times, excessive and dramatic. Madness is a spectrum within the total field of our shared becoming, sometimes an illness and at other times a protest. Madness is a wind caught in the sails of those who refuse to buckle down and yet, struggle for balance, their anchor unmoored. (23.2)

The Mystery is wind and sea and sky, earth and fire, water, stone and metal, elemental forces tossing the waves of conformity into turbulent, chaotic patterns. It is also the quiet depths of undisturbed calm whose surface activities seek to mirror that greater depth. Beyond sea and sky and earth is an Infinite Vast, an immeasurable domain in which a profound, luminous Light radiates healing Presence, healing all irruptions of madness in search of that very Light. (23.3)

Madness can be a reaction to oppression, a search for greater freedom from the blinding warp of expected behavior, duties, responsibilities unasked but given without question as shared burdens of past mentalities. A dawning new mentality must risk the turbulence of change and unexpected confrontation, to refuse conformity in the face of chaos and then to reintegrate, recover sanity in new forms, more elastic, bendable, with flexibility capable of fluid response, less stiff, more adaptive. (23.4)

Madness is a stage of transition, a loss of direction in a wilderness of social constructions not adequate to the task of transformation. The ruins of past civilizations reflect momentary greatness shadowed by war, death, and the pestilence of over-reaching pride, a tendency toward domination demanding obedience over creative freedom. Slavery is madness, superiority a mask over deep inner illness. Compassion requires true sanity—health, love, acceptance, cooperation, and partnership. (23.5)

The Mystery is transformative love growing beyond enclosed cultural attitudes that enshrine bias, prejudice, and blind uncaring as normative for collective consent. Protest is a form of hope that such blindness can be cured, that the deaf can hear, and the sick be healed. The Hermetic gift is insight that heals, restores balance, gives a new weight to center, no longer defined by the past or by biased expectations. The Mystery allows for madness without celebrating its sad necessity. (23.6)

Mystery can enshrine madness as a cloak over insights too profound to communicate, lost to those unable to see more deeply, beyond their own shadows. The shadow made by the sun is not the source of shadows; when light surrounds the opaque body-mind, darkness is made where materiality dominates. Not all madness is curable, some endures as a sign of cultural trauma, world disorder, gross imbalances, and a collective fabric of existent lies, half-truths, and stubborn denials. (23.7)

I have experienced madness, gross and subtle, losing my habituated mind in the face of vaster realities not comprehended nor acknowledged by the local collective. I have seen and heard, felt and experienced, much that is beyond words to describe, precepts and insights not suited to existing patterns of language or thought. Such encounters have required radical shifts in thinking, believing, and understanding; madness was a periodic excursus, now settled, absolved by enduring acceptance. (23.8)

The true horizons of knowledge far exceed our comprehension, ranging far beyond the borders of the acceptable, pushing us passed the known into the truly unknown, a gift of insight that can shatter a worldview and relativize all authoritative claims. Madness is a sign, a collective social indicator of cultural lack, a poignant index of our lack of deep maturity, our lack of healing abilities, a testament of cultural failure so strong that it ignites a protest against the inadequacies of complacent norms. (23.9)

Mystery seeks to overturn complacency, shrink the borders of sanity down to the actual lived, heart-felt reality of our one-on-one relationships. True cosmogenesis requires a stability whose creative, liminal agents are free to discover new precepts, insights, world-shattering revelations leading to unveiling yet more of the hidden possibilities that draws us away from past consensual ignorance and toward collective spiritualization. We seek greater sanity, not more confusion and denial. (23.10)

Madness is transitory, not enduring, a cycle reflecting limitations inwardly through personal transformation and outwardly through social awakening. Our search is for evolutionary change free from past bindings of authority based on profound social constrictions in the form of custom, law, and hierarchical order. Madness is the consequence of constriction, a forced mandate that refuses to recognize individual gifts and social potentials still buried in the detritus of inherited bias. (23.11)

Mystery holds us in the subtle embrace of our own sense of well-being, in the midst of arbitrary social and cultural contexts. We are thrown into unpredictable circumstances, and yet, Mystery is there, spirit-nurture giving us the strength and courage to overturn the unacceptable and transform the limited, opening new views of the possible without denying the value of past learning. We overcome our madness in order to give birth to sanity, health, and luminous worlds; many, not just One. (23.12)

Apocalyptic Change (24)

Change is inevitable, the entirety is in constant process, cycles, transformations, movement, flow, like the pull of gravity, never ceases. Change is a constant, like a river with long slow pools and then sudden rushing rapids; change is a chaotic induction into the unexpected. Is change, in an overall sense, directed toward a specific end, an outcome meant to epitomize the process by which it is induced? No. Change is like probability, a ratio between the possible and the unlikely. (24:1)

There are many prophecies of the end, of a great final confrontation, judgement, rewards, and condemnations. Prophetic traditions induced by male perspectives on climactic events justifying a teaching as ultimate and final. But there is no final teaching, no ultimate end, no cosmic affirmation meant to eulogize a single path. Many are the paths and many are the teachings, and none are final or absolute because all of them participate in the unending flow and change, the dynamics of the Ever Now. (24.2)

There is crisis, even apocalyptic events, like war, terrorism, death and destruction induced by weapons of mass destruction, where the true apocalypse means to "uncover, reveal, and expose" what is hidden, the unsavory motives that drive men to war, hate, and aggression. There is not one apocalypse but many, many revelations and much uncovering meant to expose deeper truth, not a doctrine or a belief, but the raw attributes that drive positive change into cycles of chaos and delusion. (24.3)

Apocalypse is not simply global or universal, but also personal and local, a matrix of beliefs and attitudes that support collective prejudices, self-defining actions, and ecstatic celebrations of the faults and failures of others. Such attitudes uncover deep insecurity, that our way is not the only way, that our beliefs are limited and partial in the face of a vast multitude of local cultures and groups. Our truths are not final or absolute, but only a shadow cast by aspirations seeking collective dominance. (24.4)

There is a sorrow in the Heart of Creation that beings feel the need to build walls against the beliefs and practices of others, even when those others demonstrate no harmful intentions. The end is not a culmination justifying a creed, because there is no such end, only a long process of dismantling illusions for a more open, creative horizon of discovery. It is the members of a given creed that must do the work of dismantling, not an outside voice, but actual believers waking to new responsibilities. (24.5)

To heal the sorrow at the Heart of Creation requires a new partnership, a communal understanding that embraces the Ever Now as the vast plenum whose diversity and density overflow all final consequences. Not one community but a far-reaching resonance between multiple communities, each pursuing the unique vision that defines their receptivity to the Infinite. A shared practice of discovery that unites a multitude of differences in the subtle light of mutual support. (24.6)

The true apocalypse is one that is promulgated by a collective whose intent is to condemn others who reject their notions of truth or justice. An apocalypse is a creation of group mind, one whose goal is to seek radical affirmations at the cost of other lives, an affirmation based in a negative, a visionary imaginal whose intent hinges upon the dualisms of saved and lost, dominant and subdued, guilty and innocence. But truth in not dual, not agonistic, but a spectrum in which duality is a minor chord. (24.7)

I know the apocalyptic, a condition that leads to unveiling, to revelations in which chaos is an active presence stirring the waters of the psyche into a morass of possible outcomes, none of which may endure, only some of which may occur. Spirit guided me through that turbulence, to a new integration of wholeness in which chaos plays a creative role. Chaos is a teacher, revealing ungrounded depths that need a secure foothold to become comprehensible, revealing quicksand not meant for crossing. (24.8)

One secure step does not always mean that we know the next one we need to take. Sometimes, there is no map, no directions, no enduring path, only an untrampled way waiting for a courageous soul to try a crossing. An apocalyptic bridge is a span of time in which chaos is the teacher and the hand rail is our lived principles providing stability in crossing over and through the turbulent flow. When the waters of life rise above a current level, we are called to rise as well, to stay afloat, to survive. (24.9)

Survival is beyond this incarnation, beyond apocalyptic dreams, beyond the chaos of change, beyond what we might call the maximum. The minimum is survival in many forms, a soul passing through the eye of the needle, our camel untied to discover new wells and water. Rebirth is an apocalypse, an uncovering of life in new forms, the burning oil is the light of soul carrying on its explorations of the maximal. An Infinite Horizon of possible becomings, not an end, but a long, unending journey. (24.10)

The Apocalypsis of our time is the radical transformation of the ordinary into the extraordinary, of the normal into the paranormal, of the spiritual into the transpiritual. We are undergoing radical collective change, confrontations with dying orders no longer suitable to a vast horizon of mutual discoveries. Beyond black and white lie not shades of gray, but a full spectrum of colors, radiant with the luminous glow of multiple hues beyond counting. There is a multispectral dawning, far beyond Apocalypsis. (24.11)

As there is no final end, but only on-going discovery, we must adapt our spiritual vision, expand the contours of our thinking to grasp an Infinite process whose purpose is the revelation of all possible worlds and kinds. In an Infinite Cosmos of beings whose awareness is shared across multiple domains of knowing, humility is the highest virtue, a realization that what we know or believe is only partial and to be free we must embrace our relative understanding and then, grow beyond its boundaries. (24.12)

PART THREE

All Conscious Love

Our love is not always conscious,
we react and embody without thought
the gift of another's presence, heedless
of the depth from which each being comes!

In a depthless ocean, discreet beings
arise and manifest on the islands
of the given, not recognizing
the Ocean that gives them
life and awareness,
not grasping the import of
a deeper knowing, that such life
expresses a profound love, a truly
conscious Being offering us
a most precious gift,
a vessel in which
the soul

Becomes a Real Being, full of
vitality, gifted beyond measure with
grace meant to bestow a capacity
for understanding, in a context
of shared awakenings where
love is a profound expression
of Inner Unity, the very
pulse of Oceanic
currents.

Holy Mother, open our hearts and minds
to that greater All Conscious Love!

Reveal the very depths
that give life to our most salient
relations, that inspire us to reach
beyond our limits, to be self-surpassing,
not grasping, not always asking,
but in quiet deliberations
to accept what is given
as a most precious
gift, life able
to love.

Why is love such a mystery?
Because You give an infinite depth
to what is possible in loving all that Is,
where the only limits are our own
unwillingness to celebrate the All as
truly worthy of deeply Conscious Love.

You challenge us to overcome our
own bias, to choose a greater task,
to identify Love as most capable
of sustaining the very cosmos
now created, enduring,
a lasting gift requiring
a deeper sentiment
of security in
Loving All.

Open our hearts to this task!
Make us ever more capable of truly
loving all that Is, of honoring
the depths of creative
shared becoming.

Holy Mother, grant
us the gift of Conscious
Love, that we may thrive,
become vessels of liquid
life poured out from an
Infinite Ocean, filled
with joyful swimmers,
as a shimmer and a
flash whose task is
to love, to learn
and then,
return!

Death, Rebirth, and Return (25)

Death is natural, not a state leading to any fearful outcome, unless we carry with us that fear into the after worlds. All afterlife is conditional, there is no final judgement, and no disposition of souls other than the life we choose and the path we follow. We can choose judgement, even suffering, but that choice is a pattern made in actual living; by embodying such beliefs, we become victims of collective fear and trauma. There are many afterlives, not one, many paths, many outcomes. (25.1)

Death is not easy but not long, more a transition and less a pitiful end. There is an end, an end to that life pattern, to that embodiment, to the formations and relations of that time and place. We cannot return in the same form, to the same place, even if we choose a rebirth in the very place of our death, there is only the old patterns now in new form. Not one old pattern but many, the layered nature of soul allows for a resurgence of past patterns, memories written into new flesh, into the ever-changing Now. (25.2)

Many lives means many deaths, many rebirths, many instances of self becoming something other, and yet, stubborn patterns persist, multigenerational bias transmits, fear and prejudice do not vanish. The sublimation of past attitudes is carried forward into circumstances that offer an opportunity for new insights and a better understanding of what is and what was. And yet, there is a continual grasping, intentions shaped by old habits, even benign attitudes that conceal a lack of insight, a lower positive. (25.3)

Many lives does not mean a greater wisdom, some patterns persist due to collective norms resistant to true grow and change. There is wisdom and it may be a unique expression of an era, but that wisdom reflects a cultural circumstance, sometimes rising above the context and something shaped by it. Many lives means that in the midst of the collective there is a possibility for new influence born out of rebirths meant to push beyond the old patterns, in search of a more grounded knowing. (25.4)

Incarnate transformations are born out of post-life discovery, the patterns transmitted within after-life are formative for what is yet to come, the forgotten past lies just below the liminal threshold, an inner urging to continue the work hidden behind the hustling flow of everyday concerns. Post-embodiment is a time of realignment, after death comes reflection, a new possible transformation if soul desires true growth in what is yet to come. There is the task of afterlife awakening, a learning still on-going. (27.5)

After-life is not simply rest, it too is a path of creative change, on-going discovery, growth in a subtle form, possible memories rekindled, across multiple lives, a search for greater insights and integration. Or simply passive unconcern, subconscious surrender to old patterns, no intent to learn, just a phase leading to the next uninspired life. Each must choose, to continue the learning process, to delve more deeply into the subtle and profound, or to continue half-awake, a somnolent soul, only partially aware. (25.6)

The form of after-life takes on the contours of the beliefs and attitudes of the post-mortem; religious is not an issue, truth is a relative expression of psychic integration. Those who live a middle-class life find a middle class after-life, those in the chaos find chaos, those with higher aspirations may find a wider variety of choices if he or she can retain conscious intent to explore. Most succumb to ordinary mindedness, imaging an afterlife in familiar patterns experienced in incarnational circumstance. (25.7)

I remember my past deaths, not all by any means, but some very distinctly, my soul leaving the body, my awareness still lucid, very self-aware, traveling into a more etheric realm, being met by angelic entities, those I once knew, strangers as well. Some transitions were rapid, others slower, but still relatively quick, a few months in incarnate time, a compulsive desire for renewal and rebirth, not always through choice, sometimes by unqualified attraction, other times by a driving intent not well understood. (25.8)

What occurs in that in-between is not necessarily profound but it offers the possibility, as in incarnate life, of learning and growing into a more self-aware being. The after-life circumstance is self-created, in harmony with other like-minded, group affinity is a strong attractor, and similarity of beliefs, a positive draw. We co-create the after-life, our shared *bardo*, by faith, by actions, by beliefs, and non-believers also cluster, atheist have their own realms, very rational and lacking in any supernatural contents. (25.9)

The fearful and anxious also have realms, as do those addicted and those impoverished by lack of awareness, mental disturbances, gross habits and violent tempers. Each goes to his or her own, not through choice but though the turning of the Wheel, the destiny of soul made by our choices and beliefs. We each create our own afterlife in concert with those who most support our beliefs, and lack of belief is just an empty slate filled by daily habits and everyday mind, just a plain ordinary after-life. (25.10)

There are others, more evolved, with higher mental or spiritual development; they are freer, less conditioned by events of death and more able to direct their after-life journey based on integral principles actually lived and practiced while embodied. The dedicated scholar may go to a scholarly realm, a scientist to a science realm, an artist to an artistic haven—if those way of life were authentic, fully practiced. Imitators or pretenders go to a world of ungrounded, unfocused, pretend imaginary. (25.11)

The higher calling is for self-awareness to recognize the after-life state as a conditional creation of former living; to let live and let go into a vaster domain far beyond the circumstantial co-creations of everyday. There are many higher realms but only reachable by spiritual refinement meant to lift the gaze above the ordinary and into a greater transpersonal horizon that is yet evolving through the very becoming of those who reach beyond the limits of everyday, open to Spirit, to the Infinite All. (25.12)

Reciprocity and Forgiveness (26)

The Buddha taught that the heart has three root poisons: greed (*raga*) supporting lust, anger (*dvesha*) supporting hatred, and ignorance (*moha*) supporting delusion. A wise teaching! The desire for more than what is necessary, more than needed, an endless more, is a form of soul inflation, a loss of grounding, a failure to discriminate between the sufficient and the surplus. The cure is letting go of appetites that only reinforce a perpetual cycle of grasping; far better to cultivate kindness and generosity. (26.1)

Greed heals through reciprocity, through sharing and community in which responsible beings take only their proper share and give surplus to those who have even less. Sharing wealth is far better than accumulating wealth, giving is better than hoarding, and selflessness is better than selfishness. Be selfless in giving! Think not of rewards but of our shared concerns for the well-being of others. Be generous, support those in need, including animals struggling for survival, be loving, not indifferent. (26.2)

Anger is the greatest source of hate, prejudice is the mark of fear against the uncertainty of others who do not share a view or belief. Religious beliefs that teach intolerance are anger-based, cultivating hatred and violence toward non-believers, a twisted spirituality based in pride and exclusive attitudes that would deny bias that contradicts the very nature of a deeper, more lucid teaching. Hatred is a fire that burns the user and scorches the community with an enflamed sense of ultimacy. (26.3)

The cure for anger and hate is compassion, love, kindness, care for the well-being of others, all others, not just one subset of others. Forgiveness is what stems from compassion, it flowers when the light of compassion nurtures growth and urges us toward opening up, sharing, caring, finding a greater depth of soul. Blame vanishes in that light because blame is a contraction around a dark center, where ill-will has fostered a corrupt attitude—compassion for others heals that buried wound. (26.4)

When compassion nurtures the heart, new roots are created, healthy soul-roots, nurtured by the deep sources of vitality and innate Being-With; the sentient depths flourish in positive florescence where love and care become primordial responses. This florescence makes responsibility light, not a weighted duty, but an overflowing fullness whose grace heals and uplifts without effort. Forgiveness may require restraint, but true responsibility expresses a spontaneous flow of love given from its deepest core. (26.5)

Ignorance and delusion fail to see the spontaneous health germinated by compassion, they miss the outcome of forgiveness, the solid connection to shared health and well-being. We heal together, not apart, we heal through consensual realizations, through new wisdom whose insights recognize wholeness in which diversity is a natural expression of creative becoming. Being-With offers us the opportunity of shared concerns, learning together in order to diversify. (26.6)

The cure of ignorance is right relations, not more learning, but a higher quality of compassion that is non-exclusive, given to all, with proper respect for what is needed and not just what is wanted. Wisdom requires discrimination, the ability to see through ignorance, to recast needs and wants into a more open frame that does no harm, that honors integrity and promises, in which there are no hidden lies or misdirection. Wisdom requires honesty, trust, and inner intentions for good partnership. (26.7)

Forgiveness is not always easy, sometimes ignorance enacted by others leaves its mark, a distressing consequence, traumatic or unresolved by stubborn resistance to any recognition of faults. I practice forgiveness and right relations, but it is a challenge in the face of others whose resistance, actions, and beliefs form a barrier to heart-centered trust. Forgiveness is not enough, a stubborn unwillingness to change blocks mutuality, forgiveness requires acceptance of the refusal of others for inner development. (26.8)

Our own forgiveness of others does not mean that others agree with our attitude or that our own values predominate over the values of those we may forgive. Often, a response demonstrates an unhealthy addiction to unexamined attitudes meant to justify abusive actions and intolerance. Authoritative thinking thrives on dominance, emotional abuse springs from the roots of irrationality, a disturbed psyche unable to control impulses, to enact mental formations long established as valid or necessary. (26.9)

The underlying condition that supports this unhealthy intolerance and emotional outbursts of blame and censure arise from old patterns, childhood circumstances, a battered life, a contracted attitude, uncentered belief in one's own worth or unworth. The healing of a sick soul requires patience, long-term dedication to responsible relations that do not seek to justify a condition but to transform it. In many cases, the resistance is so deep that only multiple lifetimes offer hope for healing. (26.10)

Wisdom, compassion, healing, love, in the collective context, all require generations of effort; the post-apocalyptic outcome is a healthy diverse set of cultural differences supporting positive mutual and global relations. This generational effort points toward the transformation of the World Soul, its growth into a stable domain supporting not just life and being, but also health and social networks of responsible, healthy individuals working in concert to heal the sick, weary, and lost. (26.11)

In a global context, of many paths and teachings, healing love is a deep well from which soul draws sustenance from the primal Source, the First Mystery, blessing us with the capacity for transformative understanding and a healing touch. The work of transformation is a spiritual task fostered and nurtured by Spirit, not just through personal efforts, but through deep attunement to deep core healing, the sacred Source that overflows our own limits and offers enduring, lasting guidance. (26.12)

Salvation and Pax Sophiana (27)

Salvation springs from knowledge, true gnosis, insight based on direct experience assimilated into a coherent understanding. Not by faith but by knowledge, such wisdom is embodied. And yet, faith matters, faith in the possibility of gnosis, that such knowledge is a true taste of What Is, an immersion in sacredness of the Ever Now resulting in profound insight concerning the heaven, earth, and humanity, all beings, each a gift of Spirit sanctified through creation and holy nature. (27.1)

Experience is the gate, but the heavenly city is unveiled through understanding of experience beyond the descriptive encounter, revealing inner intentions. The structure of the city, its forms and configurations, represents a Hermetic synthesis, a knowing whose contents is expressed through the variable aspects of its construction. Every visionary offers an image, a map or guide, but no one guide can express the ever-evolving forms that new visionaries bring to its shape and constructions. (27.2)

A heavenly city, as an image of higher order and understanding, is an evolute undergoing transformation in concert with human maturity. The more comprehensive that maturity, the more in attunement with the deeper currents of sentience, the more complex the possible forms of New Jerusalem or Hurqalya, Cities of Peace, whose inhabitants have utterly put away all weapons, lies, and self-deceptions in order to embrace a peace for all, a city for all faiths, and for all positive, loving paths. (27.3)

The Queen of that City is the divine Sophia, whose peace, the Pax Sophiana, endures beyond all apocalyptic narratives and rises above the dark clouds of war and violence for an inner radiance of healing love. The hem of Her skirt has uncountable threads, each thread descending to a soul, to the top knot of the crown, where every embodied soul feels the direct inflow of Her Presence, an invisible thread woven into multiple lifetimes and made secure through continual remembrance of Her Presence. (27.4)

The Pax Sophiana is a wisdom teaching in which human suffering is recognized as the consequence of limited desires and unexpected events; a peace that unknots the blocked flow of inner awareness and opens a horizon on the enduring truths of love, compassion, and understanding. It is a relative peace, an enduring sense of worth whose mutual benefits far outweighs the more limited advantages of personal achievements. This differentiated peace takes many forms, multiple expressions, many cities. (27.5)

But this wisdom, this peace, must be internalized through the work of personal development in concert with like-minded others, with humility not celebration. It is not a matter of flag-waving pride, but a deep grounded sense of purpose shaped by an ethos of cooperation and creative interactions. The Pax Sophiana is a feminine peace, one based on sharing and non-dominance, on allowing and supporting, fostering diversity while also teaching core values and practices. (27.6)

Pax Sophiana leads to salvation through knowledge, a knowing that recognizes that the outcomes of peace and non-violence must be earned through humility, trust, love, and intentions directed toward building such peace. This peace requires action, not simply thought or belief, but genuine efforts directed toward the healing and restitution of others, the instigation of a shared foundation. We build together or we fail together, such in the nature of enduring peace as a global reality, not just local. (27.7)

My own efforts have been directed toward education, spiritual teachings and research meant to illustrate the deeper sources of peace and wisdom as inherent to the very nature of sentient awareness. The ontologies of Sophianic wisdom reflect multidimensional and transtemporal domains whose influences continue to impact our collective understanding. Cities of Peace are a global construct whose central fountains flow with abundant sentient compassion from the very sources of Life Itself. (27.8)

As we create a more peaceful world, a network of linked centers each a radiant habitation open to creative diversity, the energy of that network will uplift minds and souls to a new comprehension. Our shared understanding is a gift that emerges out of the cocoon of our immediate personal concerns for a more open horizon in which the Pax Sophiana breaks through and radiates its deep Source, the true Ground, as sentience refined and blossoming into a vast field of brilliant forms and types. (27.9)

We barely comprehend the possibilities of the Infinite, how an entire civilization can rise and fall, never crossing the threshold to true understanding, as a collective resistance to the Greater Now. Salvation is discovery, a realization that opens a vista beyond the immediate and into the everlasting Now where form is transient but life ever-ongoing. Our deliverance from self-harm, injury, and all the myopic attitudes of material thinking, dissolve into a Greater Light, into an uncontainable All. (27.10)

The Pax Sophiana is carried by a feminine resolve to rise above the limits of patriarch, to surpass masculine authority, through a new wisdom based on stages of transformation. Sophia's light recognizes limits, has hope in shared alternate views, and celebrates co-union and partnership as the means toward lasting maturity. This peace does not surpass understanding but embodies that peace in actual relationships and in nurturing a multitude of paths representing our true diversity of soul. (27.11)

We are not one being but a multitude whose unity provides the very basis of divergence and discovery. From the One to the Many to the Multitude, such is the path and its gravity is found in the pull toward coherence, sympathy, future becoming, and a greater understanding of all that has already occurred. The horizon of peace is transtemporal, encompassing all past, present, and future becoming; salvation is the dawning knowledge of that horizon, open and receptive to billions of inhabitants. (27.12)

Parapsychic Becoming (28)

When we extend our senses beyond the physical margins, we open a horizon on a greater reality, we open to an expansive matrix of shared perceptions, sacred encounters with the dead, angelic interactions with spirits, and our relationships with Holy Spirituals. The Parapsychic Universe is one in which mind and soul reach a new psychonoetic integration, understanding dawns through the influx of light and color, through sentience extended into rich, subtle worlds of multiple etheric domains. (28.1)

This opening into the *Mundus Imaginalis*, into the Imaginal World permeated by both the physical and the spiritual, is known and sensed by psychic capacities latent to every human being. These capacities include telepathy, precognition, retrocognition, clairvoyance, psychokinesis, healing, out-of-body perceptions, post-death communication, spiritual encounters with guides, master, teacher and many other such abilities. The parapsychic domain is vast and filled with entities of many types. (28.2)

The psychic universe is real, it is far more complex than the physical world because it incorporates the material into the psychic through primary sentience, and that sentience is the medium through which psychic perception evolve and connect. The matrix of our communications, with each other, with the post-mortem, with spirits, is fostered by psychonoetic sensitivity, an awareness able to imagine, to image, see, hear, and receive guidance through subtle perceptions. (28.3)

Psychonoetic integration as "soul-knowledge" refers to our ability to engage perceptions through soul, through mindful awareness, a capacity to enter into the Imaginal, the domains in which spiritual activity is embodied by entities whose form and shape correspond to our own sensibilities of what is possible. The sentient universe is not limited to physical perceptions, as every organ of perception has a psychic aspect capable of even more refined perceptions. (28.4)

The psychonoetic spectrum sustains awareness through varying degrees of integration, our psychic abilities are an expression of that integration, not as a measure but as an overflow of potential into subtle connections with a vastly populated hyper-reality where spirits can manifest and communicate. What is required is receptivity, openness to possible communication, mythic sensitivity, psychic stability that is creative and aesthetically sensitive, a capacity for dreams, visions, and mystical intuitions. (28.5)

The parapsychic thrives through sentient affirmation when mind and heart embrace living nature as imbued with intelligence and agency, a moving power invisibly present sustaining nurture and growth. When the veil is lifted, we can see the interwoven artistry of creation through psychic connection, the weaving of patterns of soul, mind, and heart, shared and shaped by beliefs and aspirations. The impossible become possible when we can affirm its potential for actuality, believe it into being. (28.6)

I once had a vision in which I stood in an open forest bright with sunshine and I saw a lens, a large circle a meter in diameter, which floated in front of me. When I looked into the lens I could see that the forest was alive with powers and other forms of sentience, richly alive with multiple entities normally not seen outside the lens. The difference was profound, how animate parapsychic nature was, seen with more than eyes but also soul and mind united, a fusion of world and soul. (28.7)

In a later vision, I had an encounter with Phusia, an earth goddess whose radiant green form was of a young woman floating above the earth, her hair radiant and free, her robe a soft allure of feminine beauty whose heart was filled with sorrow. She showed me the abuse of nature, human ill-treatment of animals, unconcern for the primacy of nature as the Gaian-ground of life itself. I shared her sorrow, felt the fear of animals for humans, recognized the pathos of neglect shown by human indifference. (28.8)

The parapsychic reality calls us to open heart and mind and soul to the depths and fullness of the Imaginal, the in-between that nurtures all life forms beyond their physical attributes, that saturates the matrix our communications with diverse entities whose life is not reducible to imagery. Such life is subtle, co-creative, self-sustained, intelligible, with immaterial types of being. This angelic realm, spirit-born and sustained, is reachable through the Imaginal as a gift of Third Presence, Being Itself. (28.9)

The parapsychic is only an extension of sentient qualities brought to focus through sensitivity to subtle perceptions, a visionary capacity filled with reverence for the Presence that sustains, not for any one being but for all beings, all types, all forms, as the very source of our shared becoming. The ParaUniverse is a vast ocean of beings, some physical, some immaterial, some post-mortem, others beyond definitions, aliens, others worldly beings, mythic forms, and spiritual possibilities. (28.10)

We are called to enhanced perceptions, to grow beyond the ordinary into the more than ordinary, into the expression and cultivation of parapsychic abilities to affirm and share the unseen with the seen. Far beyond "mind-reading" and "mental time travel" we can open to an Infinity of layered world-becomings where beings strive to create new realities from the subtle energies of the Imaginal, co-creating beyond known forms. We can embody that creative impulse through extending perceptions into Source. (28.11)

In the parapsychic domains, there is incredible beauty, complexity, and multiple networks infused with psychic qualities that can utterly change how we see, know, and experience this world and others. Our calling is to uplift our sensibilities to new horizons of awareness in order to instill more expansive visions shared by a growing multitude, visions within visions, worlds evolved beyond materiality, becoming distinct and diverse while also knowing and embodying our unitary ground and Wholeness. (28.12)

Our Everlasting Cycles

Our great cycle is the spiral galaxy,
a slow spin made of millions of years,
a cosmic cycle, the sun's journey around
an epic mass center, a black hole,
which a billion stars also
cycle, each with its own
barycenter, a flux,
a stabilizing
motion.

Cycles are everywhere, a spinning sun,
rotating planets, moons, comets
a holy work of constant motion
vibrant with celestial vibration,
a Harmony of Spheres
resonant with
deep musical
diverse
tones.

Sentience pervades the All, everything
alive, the Creative Intent expressed
in cycles of becoming, in the
patterns of nature, in the
turning earth, in seasons,
in the flux and flow
of birth and death,
an unending
Process.

Holy Mother blessed is your creative Power!
Miraculous the complexity of the Whole!

Our refinement through repetition, through cycles
that spiral not as self similar, but each cycle
adding nuance, diversity, difference, an
evolution based in creative repetitions
differentiated by maturity and
increasing insights, made
real by actualizations,
the opening of our
Inner Eyes.

Beyond the lineal, lies the cyclical,
Beyond the line, lies the circle,
Beyond the circle, lies the
Tesseract, a Penteract,
A Nine-Cube, a Hyperdimensional
dynamic, not a shape but a cycle
of transformation leading
to ever richer forms,
ever more complex
expressions of Becoming,
to an Ever Now whose
dimensional being
far exceeds the
ordinariness of
perception.

We are called to these higher perceptions
to multidimensional Being, through
the spiral path of collective cycles;
it is a spiritual realization that
must be refined. Holy Spirit
shining through vertices
of cosmic plurality, an
Awakening much

to be desired
Always!

Bless us and Guide our path!

The Ever Enduring Now (29)

The Now is all time gathered into a Gordian Knot, a complex weave of multiple temporal strands whose tangle is only an appearance, an ordered complexity in which the lineal is a strand, a personalized perspective meant to give structure to a formless All. If we break the symmetry, free ourselves from the necessity of past-present-future, then we begin to recognize the true complexity of the Ever Now, enfolded orders of creative change and developmental strands, no longer predictable, only probable. (29.1)

The Ever Now is multidimensional, multi-spatial Being, a vast complexity of domains not understood or even conceptualized beyond mathematical formulas. Not abstract space but lived-space, replete with influences across the branes, subtle energies, psychic influences, metacosmic interactions penetrating the foam of quantum interactions. An entangle universe, or multiverse, of cocreated domains best connected through mind and soul, as elemental participants in the cosmic dance. (29.2)

There are no frozen forms, only the long enduring dynamics of uncountable stars each a point in the multi-spatial field, linked together in galactic harmonies of conjoined stellar awareness. Long duration does not mean unchanging, rather the slow evolute of stellar particles enlivening all celestial bodies, human as well as a multitude of others. The cycles of birth and death references even the stars and galactic formations, holospheres, near galactic forms, distant other forms, strange energies, some dark. (29.3)

The multidimensional, transtemporal cosmos has shifted all old concepts of cosmos, we are not the center; perhaps there is no center other than the galactic core of every stellar formation. A multicentric cosmos, all in motion, expansion and contraction, the rhythmic pulse of creation, a vastness so great as to be incomprehensible, and humanity a unique species on the fringe of only one galactic form, yet sustaining multidimensional beings, able to awaken and to participate in cosmic wonder. (29.4)

The Ever Now is the present moment of awareness, the immediate embodied sense of clear perception resonant with individual predispositions. It is always Now, no before or after other than through memory or probability, the ever-expansive, enduring Now extended into the Infinite as myriad possibilities contracted to the mind and heart of the perceiver. Our relative perceptions only hint at the true scope of the Ever Now because it requires an opening of mind far beyond the ordinary to full apprehend. (29.5)

Imagine standing on a mountain, a clear evening sky, lucid and colorful; your eyes see the distant horizon, the vast space above, the first stars dawning. Now imagine a hypervision in which you see the energies and flow of consciousness in a World Soul context, the living presence of shared awareness. Now lift your vision to the heavens and see there a vast cosmos of intercommunicating worlds, each full of life and open to direct mind-to-mind communication. Such is the Ever Now, a vast expanse across the Void. (29.6).

There is birth, life, and death in the Ever Now, all creatures undergoing change through cycles of becoming, centered in the Now moment as events and persons process through the Gate of Transformation, beyond which the Ever Now reveals the promise that we are participants in cosmic revolutions meant to unveil possible truths. In the Ever Now all truths are possible but those that endure sanction life over death and species transformation over contracted withdrawal. (29.7)

I was lifted to the Ever Now by a wave, not one but multiple waves, each a surge that broke through my pattered thoughts to reveal a cosmos unbound by mental attitudes and resonant with life-vitality, awareness, and intelligibility. It strengthened my heart, held me suspended in a deep connection through which Intelligible Being showed me a vastness far beyond my comprehension. But there was comfort, joy, peace, a sense of purpose through which I could conceive a better future for humanity. (29.8)

The Ever Now has no boundaries, no beginning and no end, it is the enduring truth of present-centered existence, as long as there is cosmos, there is Ever Now. When time slows or reverses or increases its tempo, the Ever Now remains constant; inconstancy is a human tendency to grasp a present or past or future moment as more meaningful than the actual present Now. But this grasping tendency simply magnifies a concern meant to illustrate a tendency to interpret What Is in a specific frame. (29.9)

We continually frame the present in terms of past and future, a natural attitude, but one bracketed by lineal time, frames stacked to create an ordered montage, to reveal underlying patterns. Historical knowledge is present-centered, what happened then or what will happen, only endure in the Now; we understand a past event only in the ever-changing present, everything abides in the Now as we discover meaning in the hidden patterns, unveil a tendency, illuminate an attitude active in the ever-enduring Now. (29.10)

We can expand our experience of the Now into a much vaster horizon that incorporates an ever-increasing number of domains, dimensions, or worlds. Blesséd is the Now as a testimony of the sacred ground through which all beings become; a profoundly complex Reality whose processes reflect the Life Principle at every level of organization. We are radiant with life, intelligence, love, compassion, and beauty, if we only open our hearts to the Now in all its complex designs of sacredness. (29.11)

The Timeless Now is also a true existent, not beyond temporal flow but in the midst of temporal discovery; the timeless Present is no different than the temporal moment. Everything we see and know, every being and form, is participant in the timeless concatenation of Being-With, together we endure the Infinite by recognizing our limits and individuality. Change occurs and the wheel turns, nothing is static. (29.12)

World Soul, World Awakening (30)

There is a heart-beat in the World Soul, a rhythm whose pulse reflects the stages of our shared evolution toward true awakening. The beat is not always steady, at times erratic, shuttered, too fast, as cultures collide and wars and reprisal dominate global relations. The World Soul does not thrive on excess, it seeks balance, shared responsibilities, cooperative networks of co-workers able to stabilize without bias, to overturn dominance into a more dynamic, partnered, balanced wholeness. (30.1)

World awakening is difficult, there is no one path forward and there is a dangerous fracture when surface consciousness collapses into a myriad of discreet subgroups, all clamoring for recognition. This fragmented contestation reveals a lack of integration as cultural members reiterate the biases of past generations and seek to impose their views on others who think and believe differently. When those biases collapse, social chaos breaks out, lies and truth mix, and skepticism dominates. (30.2)

There is a painful truth in this collapse of dominant worldviews. In the chaos of the collapse, it becomes increasingly clear that early communal, conservative human attitudes and practices have dominated, based on a fictive history of superior values meant to justify oppression, violence, slavery, and the denial of the rights of others. This is not a matter of abstract ideas but of cultural practices causing great harm to major populations in the name of truths claimed to be absolute. (30.3)

In religions, sciences, political organizations, and other cultural institutions, this attitude is profoundly evident, a belief in the legitimacy of a particular set of values that represent a biased past, benefits for the few, an aristocracy of belief justifying social and economic dominance in the name of higher ideals. When these attitudes are challenged, begin to collapse, revealing injustice, falsehoods, and manipulation, then the reaction is often violent and aggressive. Peace requires maturity, not only resistance. (30.4)

The World Soul is a construct of human thought and emotive

mentality, it is based on psychic collusion uncontrolled by any one culture or nation. It is a natural psychic process stimulated by increased populations, electronic communication, and increasing access to a knowledge base far exceeding the capacity of any individual or group to integrate. Every area of study, every scientific discovery, every exploration of culture, every literary production, every image, thought or idea, contributes. (30.5)

The psychosynthesis of thought worlds, the inhabitation of alternative cultures, the exploration of cosmic space, deep ocean dives and high-flying solar vistas all contribute. The multicosm reveals an unending litany of possible worlds, beings, and transformations manifesting and the molecular, genetic, and social levels of human experience all support the arising of a World Soul—a share subtle interactive global sphere encompassing and supporting all mentalities and thought forms. (30.6)

The World Soul is not a moral entity; it is a field that reflects our species wide relationships, including all other species, as a co-creative sphere whose purpose or direction of development depends upon each and every individual. Our social formations, organizations, institutions, and fraternal and sororal groups all offer psychic influences in the on-going dynamics of World Soul development. In a process view, this development is contingent upon the actually existential value of each person. (30.7)

As an ancient entity, the World Soul has evolved in direct concourse with all species development. I know this entity; I have experienced its global scope and dimensions as part of a much large construction between worlds. Billions of living beings, human and other, support and embody its defining characteristics but the scope of that field far exceeds our local world, charged by the subtle energies of our star, a link in an astral network whose inhabitants shape many other World Souls. (30.8)

All species contribute, the World Soul is an energetic formation sustaining every life form as intrinsic to a total field of relations. In so far as we treat all species with respect, non-violence, and partnership, the World Soul thrives. But when we act as predators, dominating and slaughtering other species, the World Soul contracts and suffers the fracturing disharmonies of habituated mentalities addicted to personal appetites and mental attitudes distaining the value and worth of other creatures. (30.9)

World Awakening requires a new ethos of co-species existence, responsible care for the well-being of every species and, to the best of our ability, to promote interspecies harmony and enrichment. This means ecological actions and choice that support environmental health and balance, as a sustainable future for World Soul development. A healthy world reflects healthy souls; culture wars must cease and cooperation must support a new ethos of shared responsibilities based on positive spiritual values. (30.10)

World Awakening is not a predetermined process; it evolves through consensual attitudes, conditional ethos, and values promulgated through social practices. If the attitudes, ethos, and practices contract around self-serving, aggressive dispositions, the habitation of the World Soul is contracted. A World Soul can flourish or fixate, expand or contract, open or close in relationship to communal embodiments. A predatory world will collapse, forming a lower world, closed to the Infinite. (30.11)

A mature World Soul embraces diversity, supports all species, preserves life and eco-habitats in a context of respect, appreciation, and reverence. All beings matter, none too small or insignificant; humanity is not the dominant species, but a partner whose stewardship promotes and fosters the gift of life in all forms. When the World Soul opens to the Infinite then new populations form, linking worlds, stars, a galactic communion across the void in a profound network of shared worlds and beings. (30.12).

Prophecy and the Future (31)

Future becoming is based in probability, possible pathways forward without predetermination, relative possible futures, open to change and purpose. Prophecy is an intuitive inspiration, a gift of insight, rising out of those probabilities, forming a visionary outcome. Prophetic insight is born out of Being-With, not from becoming, but from the core attributes the represent the prophetic ideal. Prophecy is ontological, a witness testimony of a possible path, intuitive assessment, not a specific future. (31.1)

Prophecy is not precognition, it is not about prediction or future events; prophecy is rooted in a stance, an existential commitment to a way of life, based in social and cosmic values. The prophetic ideal is variable but in each case, there are core values which represent spiritual goals, an integrated community of followers who embody the ideal in proximal forms. The prophetic testimony is a call to those devotees to better embody the ideal, to increase purposeful existence through actualizations. (31.2)

The Hermetic ideal is gnosis, direct experiential knowing, refined through interpretation and embodied in core values meant to epitomize a cooperative, shared world of responsible, loving relationships. It is a path of the heart, a Sophos Ontology whose purpose is to embody visionary potential as real and actual through generational development. It is not a call to worship but an invocation of Presence, an embodied illumination, and a lasting, enduring, life-long testimony of commitment. (31.3)

The Hermetic ideal is like a Grail quest, not a search for an object, but for an immersive understanding; to drink from the Grail cup means to imbibe the living waters of sacred Presence, to hear holy words as inspiring thoughts. The Grail serves each and every seeker, stands forth as an emblematic sign, like a dove carrying an olive branch, perched on an ever-blooming almond tree. The tree signifies health, the olive branch, fruitful peace, and the dove, a Holy Spiritual manifestation. (31.4)

The future is dark and cloudy, in the near view, an over-burdened population, disease, hunger, constant migrations, and excess wealth unshared by those in need. The farther future appears also cloud-covered, awaiting the birth of a new global intelligence, now in the throes of birth. There is contestation, more wars, death as a result of indifference to the gift of life, a predatory sense of dominance seeking control through violence. All caught in the throes of contraction, the struggle for rebirth. (31.5)

And yet, the far future seems radiant, a high water world of fewer beings at peace after a long struggle, reduced to the very core values that inspire a lasting spiritual realization. This is not prophecy, only intuitions and visions of probable becoming, a far future surviving the traumas of evolution to attain a new stage of Being. And how is this new stage attained? Through commitment and embodiment of genuine spiritual ideals; through processes of discovery and a willingness to learn from other paths. (31.6)

The Hermetic ideal is only one path among many, there is no exclusive "one way"—such attitudes must pass away in the evolution of new becomings. There are many paths whose member and practitioners can work together to form networks of value and actions contributing to World Soul development. We are each a path, we can have affinity and membership in multiple groups, traditions, and communities, where synthesis is a testimony for the prophetic ideal we each embody. (31.7)

My own path has many influences from diverse traditions, multiple religions, scientific research, humanistic studies, philosophical alternatives, and paranormal investigations. I call my path Hermetic as a sign, a prophetic witness to an esoteric stream of wisdom teachings realized through a multitude of individual practitioners. But there is nothing exclusive in such a path, all teachings are part of the Book of Life, each chapter a different vision of the Whole. All cultures contribute, all wisdoms shared. (31.8)

The future is made, not predetermined, it is a choice, a collective synthesis whose outcomes remain probable, not certain, not apocalyptic, unless we choose destruction, indifference, and dominance over compassion, love, and wisdom. We are each a determinant, an anchor when well-disposed and caring, a flotsam when we drift with every current, and an obstacle where we hold stubbornly to half-truths and delusions. Each person is a node in the shared mentality of evolutionary becoming. (31.9)

Prophetic truth depends upon the community of a given ideal, not as abstract prediction, but through embodied practices, to illustrate higher values that lead to peace, cooperation, and new life. If the ideal promotes war, oppression, censure, condemnation, and violent actions, it is a path less worthy, dangerous, and suffering from a deep inferiority as to its worth and value. The enduring path is open and adaptive, not closed and blaming; what endures is flexible, many sided, multidimensional, vast. (31.10)

While there are many Prophetic ideals, there is a common ground, rooted in an enduring God-sense, in a fertile, dark soil capable of ever-more creative realizations. If we strip away the cultural dress, the historical moment, and contextual eco-sphere, then we see not an essence, but a living Presence so vibrant and profound that is can take ten million forms and still offer Infinitely More. This Presence overspills all forms and manifestations, in, around, and beyond form, the Birth Mother of all beings. (31.11)

The future has yet to become, it is still in process; in the Ever Now, the future vanishes into a much more complex, multidimensional Reality whose outcomes allow for multiple future becomings, all held in the sacred embrace of Spirit, First Mystery, Being-With, as possible Spheres of Knowing, awaiting discovery and expression. What will Be and what will Become await our individual and collective decisions. For the Hermetic Ideal, the prophetic future remains elusive, possible, and promising. (31.12)

The Metacosmos Unveiled (32)

What is the Metacosmos? It is all visible and invisible domains of all conscious beings throughout all space and time, as nurtured within atemporal and transpatial Being. It is the living universe held within the All God-Light Present; like a stone in the bottom of the sea, the visible is surrounded and saturated by currents, domains, dimensions of the timeless, immortal, sentient Ocean of the Ever Now that cannot be confined to mind or image or thought. (32.1)

The Metacosmos is found where thought meets the impassable notion of the Infinite, as words ascend toward Its vastness, the heart contracts to everydayness; and yet, expansion and contraction are the rhythms of life, found in the pangs of childbirth, the punctuated equilibrium of day and night, waking and sleeping, knowing and not-knowing. It is a promise that all we see is not all that Is, what we know is not all that can be Known. (32.2)

Recovery of the Metacosmos is inseparable from the recovery of the soul; perceptions of the heart expand into the many domains of all-conscious life, a unitary intersection of individual, collective, and hyper-collective perceptions built on the slender scaffolding of our desires and aspirations. As soul develops, the domains of perception expand, opening to an intersected universe of multiple possible worlds, into an Ur-Space containing all living beings across all gravity wells of time and world becoming. (32.3)

I cannot comprehend the Metacosmos, I can only hold the vision as it comes to me, unbidden, like a wave of magnificent beauty, uplifting beyond form and crashing back into individual embodiments. In pools of vanishing light that expand through multiple worlds, I see the subtle that surrounds the gross, the invisible that permeates the solid, the radiance that imbues all substances with life-held-vitality, that nurtures in the most minute, the possibility for the More. (32.4)

The Metacosmos includes all cosmologies, all theories of Astro-Cosmological conception, all imaginings of religion, art, and science, all worldviews that would explain the origins or creations of the visible, the invisible, and the in-between. Each vision, each creation narrative, each science theory, is only another pool, another circle within the intersecting circles of an Infinite that has no end, as each offers a unique meaning that encompasses a way of life or a vision of the possible. (32.5)

These visions exist in complementary relations within the Metacosmos, each holding its own seeds of sentient truth in relation to human need, as images of the whole whose vitality is embodied in shared and collective values, each growing and mutating through the influence of other worlds and views, through the power of creative Spirit who fosters the communion of souls at the heart of each world; only together can they represent a Whole whose circumference cannot be measured. (13.6)

Endless symbols, designs, languages, and expressive forms reflect the Metacosmos as modest images of a Whole that cannot be transcribed; the full spectrum of the Metacosmos includes all energies, all wave signs, all happenings in all domains, as seen and known through the spectral vision of each life form, given its unique flavor, taste, texture, and qualities according to the bound perceptions inherent to each individual life, however gross, subtle or immaterial. (32.7)

These views do not clash as much as intersect and highlight unique features of the possible within the context of the actual; in the Metacosmos there is no Final Theory of Everything, other than those theories embraced by a minority who claim ultimacy in the name of relative and partial sciences. There is no final theory because within the ParaUniverse such theories must incorporate the ever-evolving sentient Whole, all psychic, spiritual, and transpersonal domains, not simply material-energetic processes. (32.8)

Within these domains, there is emergence and discovery, creative innovation and artistic expression, articulation and formulaic utterances surpassing the What that has already been. That which becomes is capable of change even at the base level of material-energetic processes, where mind intersects matter, miracle is possible, where soul intersects with energy, revelation can occur, where love permeates body, transformation can unfold and give birth to new worlds and forms. (32.9)

In the Metacosmos, creative transformation is the medium of sentient beings in relation to the Whole, in the mental, imaginative, visionary domains of the in-between, the *Mundus Imaginalis*, the fertile fields of the World Soul, within the hyper-conscious continuum that links our world with a multitude of others. Across the spectrums of the Infinite, ever-present and alive, information flows, a million streams into an ocean without shores, nourishing life, Holy Spirit Mother given. (32.10)

True *gnosis*, visionary knowledge, begins when the veils of the ParaUniverse are raised to reveal the vast, interwoven complexity of all possible worlds vibrant with life and awareness; within these many fields of life and world-habitation, countless beings attain insight and illumination, each a reflected jewel within the ever-undulating net of the enfolded continuum between worlds. The lightening along the strands of that net creates the ever-evolving matrix that constitutes profound mystical transformations. (32.11)

Every transcription of the Metacosmos is a sign, not of its breadth and depth, but of the limitations and capacities of the transcriber, the relative homing of the individual, the local immersion of each visionary in the context of a world saturated system of ideas and beliefs. This knowledge is relative and yet, truly visionary; contextual and yet, transpersonal; true, yet partial in the over-arching totality of what is and may become, surpassed by the generations of visionaries yet to come. (32.12)

Blessing Songs New Sung

Every singer has a song, and
every song has melody,
a musical harmonic
reflecting the soul,
some joyful, some sad,
melancholy, more a wobble
or warble, seeking to express
rooted, deeply held emotions.

Our blessing songs are not simple
celebrations but also refractions of
soul life, illustrating a struggle to
creatively body-forth an aspect,
plane, dimension, an angle
of perception welding a
shard of light to
physical form,
soulfully!

We are multidimensional beings in a
vast cosmos of interdimensional
domains, a multitude of others
some subtle, less seen, but
actively alive and present;
all expressing a finesse
of ensouled forms
as multiaxial
Being-With.

Holy Mother, Blesséd Father, Holy Children!

One great plurality, a multitude of network
relations, sharing a common struggle
to express the Infinite in actual
specific attributes, a synthetic
syntropy, a creative matrix,
multiple beings seeking
salvation through
genuine gnosis,
direct insight
into Ever
Now.

We sing our songs, write our poems,
hear the lullaby in the wind as a testimony
of shared interactions, a harmonic flux
whose intentions seek to express
being-awareness, opening to
enduring Source whose
Presence gives us the
gift-of-life, the
most sacred
treasure!

Love,
wisdom, patience,
purity, empathy, care,
joy, hope, sorrow, and sacrifice
all contribute to a vaster becoming
whose deep influences rise above surface
life, revealing a vista, a horizon of possibilities
requiring our utmost attention and effort to actualize.
The foundation of our efforts is multiplex Being, the
very Source, the inexhaustible heart, ever-beating.

Holy Mother, may your inspiration ever reign
as a call to evolutionary health and well-being!
May we become more nuanced, ever more
expressive of the sources of our shared
inspirations, collated for the good
of all beings, aesthetic works,
artful forms, beauty new
shaped, joy and hope
the sisters of new
discovery for
all beings!

Selah!

Higher Intelligence (33)

Intelligence is a gift, given over many generations, shared across species, and a consequence of past choices and actions. There are multiple intelligences, many ways in which learning and education contribute to intelligible knowing. No one form or type of intelligence is superior as all intelligence is relative to its use and application. Intelligence is an expression of insight, artistic, mathematical, scientific, or spiritual. Specialized knowledge is a fraction of the entire field of cross-disciplinary knowing. (33.1)

Genetics, neurology, and social context can all influence intelligence, like intuition and empathy, intelligence is difficult to define and local bias permeates intelligence evaluation. Mathematical intelligence is not the same as moral intelligence, spiritual understanding is not the same as scientific investigation. Each kind of intelligence has its own field of operative conditions, a context in which thoughtfulness seeks to illumine an area of experience or study, a way to deepen insight. (33.2)

Genius has its own context, a spontaneous ability, often unique and specific to an individual, a gift of insight concerning various areas of interest. Such abilities are not universal, they represent special examples of what is possible in term of immediate understanding. The Infinite Now exceeds even the greatest intelligence and yet, is the very source of such intelligibility. Like a spring feeding diverse rivulets, intelligibility is a primal aspect of sentient Being, therefore, all intelligence has sacred roots. (33.3)

The most profound intelligence is not measurable, it is like diving into the structure of matter only to find vast energies part of entangled networks whose local expression connects across an immense ocean of other possible forms. True Higher Intelligence is transhuman, that is, beyond human norms and expectations, because it expresses the very nature of Super-Existent Being. What we see in human form, genius or not, is only a fraction of that Greater Intelligibility nurturing all human types. (33.4)

The sacred sources of intelligence come out of sentient awareness in its most basic forms; even at the sub-molecular levels, intelligence creates bonds between particles, relationships responsive and reactive to conditional circumstances. Through increasing complexity, intelligences becomes ever-more embedded, embodied, enactive, and extended, forming conditional beings whose depth and creative becoming reflect something deeper than simple cognition. (33.5)

Every species reflects intelligence, the unique conditional awareness that promotes positive comprehension of situational location, relations with others, and place and role in an ecological context. We are all inseparably part of both local and global conditions that require intelligence for creative development, survival, and the ability to flourish in partnership with all others. A key feature of intelligence is the ability to recognize our role in relationship to the Whole. (33.6)

Because there are many different types of intelligence, there is little consensus in the evaluation of higher intelligence. Higher in what sense? In theory? In application? In practice? In social relations? In spiritual insight? Each are relevant and our capacity for evaluation is itself a reflection of intelligence. Persons tend to understand the world in terms of the degree of their own intelligibility. Like unto like is common, whereas like unto unlike is rare; we take our own measure as a yardstick for measuring others. (33.7)

Higher intelligence is elusive, because it is a creative expression entangled with abilities and talents unique to the individual; my own abilities are only relative to those of others and there is no absolute measure of what is possible in intelligent awareness. The idea of Higher Intelligent is not a set of qualities or a testable feature of awareness, but a unique synthesis whose realizations correspond to the aspirations and focus of the aspirant; the results are what matters, what is shared, communicated, and realized. (33.8)

Higher Intelligence is a qualitative development based in primary mental and emotional habits, where emotional intelligence is as important as mental acuity. The intelligence of the heart is different than intelligence of the mind; my own approach to intelligence values heart-felt perception as authentic expressions of ontological insight, not rationalized but experientially validated through actual living, intersubjective relations, love and kindness, a felt sense of the Whole and its sacred Ground. (33.9)

Intelligence is variable and conditional, reactive and responsive, analytic and synthetic, syntropic and intuitive. It expresses knowing, understanding, comprehension based in a direct realization of spiritual depth and fullness encompassing and extending beyond the range of normal physical perceptions. Higher intelligence is a consequence of a breakthrough into the Super-Existent domains, a realization that has a vast field of possible knowledge-fields, spheres of knowing requiring multimodal insights. (33.10)

There is a psychic aspect to Higher Intelligence, as it is not based on facts or calculative reasoning, but on an immediacy of unitary perceptions intrinsic to the larger Holosphere, to a World Soul orientation, that values the Whole as inseparable from the individual. We perceive this Wholeness in and through our deepest psychic capacities, a form of soul-knowledge, a direct experiential grounding in the sacred All, in the Ever Now, in the unique configurations of individual perception. (33.11)

Higher Intelligence evolves and develops through generational patterns—religious, scientific, cultural, international, global. These patterns are prophetic concerning the consequences that emerge, prefiguring a variety of outcomes based in the application of that intelligence. Spirituality is an outcome of such intelligence, not free from bias or preferences, not absolute in an enduring sense, and highly relative to the intelligences of others. Spiritual intelligence is an evolute, still in process. (33.12)

Art, Music, Poetry (34)

Aesthetic expression has diverse centers of gravity, for some it is an expression of beauty, for others a form of social criticism, or a stylistic concern or a trend whose cultural matrix shapes audience response. Aesthetic expression is intrinsic to every religious and spiritual traditions as an artful means to communicate the vision embodied by a participant artist. And every artist has his or her own unique understanding of that tradition and its core values. (34.1)

Icon paintings, Buddhist sculpture, religious architecture, choral music, mandala making, costumes, and shamanic dance all express the aesthetic impulse. Some art is more sacred and some more secular but the impulse comes from a soul-source that reflects the uncanny depths of psychic life made explicit. Deep art, not just popular surface expressions, alludes to our connection with the World Soul, not through faith or belief, but through the actions of creative, aesthetic expression. (34.2)

The creative impulse can take many artistic forms, and spirituality benefits from that impulse when it expresses both aural, tactile, and visual forms meant to inspire and guide understanding to new perspectives. Art is not simply about pleasure but pleasure has a place in spirituality as a conduit for enjoyment of aesthetic forms. Zen painting or haiku, a Catholic mass or Gregorian chant, Sufi dance or dhikr, the songs of Rosh Hashanah or shofar, the poetic rhapsody of Qur'an all express soulful qualities. (34.3)

In many ways, music and poetry are more direct than explanations or theologies, philosophical reflections cannot rise to the more subtle heights of poetic verse or the inspiring uplift of musical tones and cadence. Artful forms, painting or sculpture, have captured spiritual teachings in transverbal media irreducible to wordy explanations; the immediacy of art is sensory and transensory, directness of perception deeply felt, a sense of the sacred by-passing description for participant knowing. (34.4)

Beauty is not a minor concern, it is a core principle, emanating from the heart of creation and manifest in a vast multitude of life forms, in creaturely forms brilliant with color, design, adaptive camouflage, and ecological fitness. The cosmos itself is an aesthetic expression of balance in a context of creative chaos; moon, sun, stars, or galaxy, are all harmonic forms each with their own secret depths, an inner beauty of creative power and sacred presence, harmonizing within the ever expanding One Life. (34.5)

Beauty as a principle of life manifest in every species, it is not an abstract ideal, but a living presence seen in the animal, plant, aerial, aquatic, insect, mineral worlds, in elemental nature, and in the mystery of entangled harmonic, quantum resonance. The interconnectedness of species and world is an expression of intrinsic balance whose dynamic is vulnerable to the unbeautiful behavior of sentients bent on profit, production, and the perilous abuse of worldly materiality. (34.6)

The artful expression of beauty includes the atonal, the surreal, the imaginal possibility extended beyond conventional forms, something far more than classical. The dark side of beauty is its use in the manipulation of others leading to false desires and artifice only as surface shadow play. Deep beauty stems from the creative matrix giving birth to visions not limited by current popularity but based in the absorbing matrix of ontological expression, Being made aesthetically apparent. (34.7)

Poetry and music are two expressive forms whose resonance

has long influenced my own development; the music of language and the language of music correspond to feelings and perceptions uncontainable in descriptive words. Music lifts the soul and poetry hones awareness of the subtle and differentiated; paintings open a world of imagery and sculpture bodied forth inner vision. Dance and mime reveal bodily expressions, theatre and drama can engage a full range of perceptual response. (34.8)

Music is one of the most profound of all aesthetic expressions, opening new dimensions in soundscapes beyond structure. Whatever the mode—primal, subtle, rhythmic, driven or expansive—music carries a reverberation that penetrates to the very heart of creation. Music of the spheres points toward cosmological harmonics, subtle undertones convergent across wide domains of open space, a sounding note uncontained in three-dimensional awareness. I hear this music directly, with mind and heart open. (34.9)

The visual arts, material or electronic, are also a stimulus to spiritual development, the phenomenology of lived-world perception is grounded in imagery, and in sound, touch, taste, and smell as well as many other sensory modes. Imagery feeds the imaginal and the real as a single continuum in which outer world objects transmit through imagery into inner world constructions. The aesthetic mode refines that process of internalization by inducing reflection upon its aesthetic aspects. (34.10)

We learn to see the good or the beautiful through mental sensitivities cultivated in part by aesthetic perceptions internalized through imagery reflecting artful ideals. Meditation on visual art forms, mandals, iconic images, archetypes, all contribute to soul sensitivity, coupled with harmonic sound and mental stillness, enhancing the aesthetic response. The Imaginal reflection on aesthetic expressions can enhance spiritual awareness if the imagery communicates inner values to the meditator. (34.11)

The Good or Beautiful as a spiritual ideal is an expression of direct experience insofar as we are able to engage the World Soul at the deep level of its perfectibility. Not because we become perfect, nor that the World Soul is perfect, but because perfectibility is a developmental process based on positive intent and cooperative concerns aimed at producing a balanced, harmonious spiritual communion of persons committed to being good and beautiful as expressed in their actions, thoughts, words, and deeds. (34.12)

Creative Ontologies (35)

Hermetic Illumination is based in true "love of wisdom" (philosophy) through direct engagement with ideas, teachings, and schools of thought without giving exclusive allegiance to any one approach. This means that wisdom has many forms, many schools of thought, and many mental and spiritual dispositions that create a context for learning. At the heart of this praxis is *gnosis*, genuine knowledge based on direct perceptions, variable, diverse, and individual. (35.1)

While there is a universal ontological ground, a sacred basis for the arising of sentience, intelligibility, moral conscience, and aesthetic expression, a mystical ground providing a vast context for types of realization, no one expression or school can capture the finesse and differentiations actually experienced by individual gnosis. Universal ground and individual realizations lead to communities of faith that embody that universal ground, as distinct from other equally valid spiritual communities. (35.2)

Thus, there are many spiritual communities who claim a valid teaching, fully expressive of variable types of beliefs and forms of knowledge, often rationalized in accord with founding principles. While such a community may exclaim the universal nature of their teachings, such claims are relative to the claims of other communities who also support a universal ground. Many paths, many teachings, many alternatives, all stemming from a common universal ground, a mystical garden of many blooms. (35.3)

We may have preferences, say a rose rather than a lily, but that does not make the preference superior to other teachings or flowers. A lesser bloom may offer unique insights while larger blooms may be more visible, the small, the minute, the tiny, also have characteristics worthy of study. Common attitudes often reflect surface views, a teaching glossing over problematic aspects of deeper sources. Every teaching has imperfections, reflecting the understanding and bias of its authors. (35.4)

Even the greatest teachers and teachings are relative to the teachings of other equally great teachers. There is no greatest teacher, no specific path meant for all peoples, every community has its own teachers and instructions. The greater teachings acknowledge diversity and difference without hierarchical judgements, able to appreciate the merits and value of other points of view. The fundamental principle is simple—no one perspective accommodates all possible views. (35.5)

There is ontological entanglement, a metaphysics of accommodation that values plurality as significant as unity, while also acknowledging a common metastable ground of Infinite depths and possibilities. If that ground is capable of infinite forms, no one form can fully express its actual potential except through variable creative occasions in a process of unending discovery. And yet, that ground is stable, a sentient fullness whose intelligible aspects promote differentiation as a means to ontological realization. (35.6)

The goal is not a grand synthesis, a metatheory meant to accommodate all possible forms, but instead a spiritual practice aimed at the realization of specific forms. The Hermetic Gnosis is one such form, a spiritual point of view in the midst of finite other points of view. The spiritual practice is direct engagement with the metastable ground, what I call Super-Existent Being, as a form of revelation in a direct personal sense; the task is to articulate and share that emergent, individual perspectives. (35.7)

Our shared ontological depths come to be known through the processes of direct encounter, self-reflections, communal synthesis, and historical discoveries challenging the limitations of a given view. Through genuine gnosis, I see and know that Depth as an endless potential for spiritual actualizations, knowing also the limitations of my own awareness. And yet those limitations represent the very boundaries that define an individual perspective, valid and actual through lived experience. (35.8)

A universal ground supports our differences and accommodates our personal development in relationship to the experiences and learning of others, as well as our lived relationship to the Whole. This is not a realization acquired through thought or mental constructions, but a soulful heart-centered aspiration to embody the very qualities we recognize as most valuable for an authentic spiritual life. To actualize the ideal requires our utmost efforts, thought alone cannot achieve this realization. (35.9)

There are many diverse, creative ontologies because beings are capable of diverse understandings; there is no convergence or necessary sublimation of other ontological expressions, they live or die in accord with the values and insights they provide. What endures is the source matrix, the Infinite Ground, whose pluripotent capacities overflow all normative limits and provoke an aspiration to greater illumination and insight. There are no final states, only the long, complex process of developmental discovery. (35.10)

Diverse ontologies teach us an important lesson, that complexity is a feature of ontological diversity, not because a systemic view is complete but because it represents a possible synthesis. Every enduring synthesis reflects ontological engagement as a lifetime practice, gradual realizations punctuated by sudden insights, the application of unitary ground in multiple subjectivities—all contributing to a unique point of view. Great thinkers offer specific views, their truth, not the only Truth. (35.11)

Philosophies are like musical compositions, with many forms and melodies, many great orchestrations, symphonies of astonishing depth, feeling, and mastery—and many simpler tunes uplifting and memorable. Every composition adds to the complexity of the Whole, there may be schools, movements, orders, but those also add to the complexity. The greater resonance is found within the harmonic tones sustained by the All, in which every note, word, thought, and image manifests the Abundant Fullness. (35.12)

Re-Becoming Again (36)

The cycles of life are unending, a continuous repatterning through embodied experiences followed by death, transition, and rebirth. Each new birth recreates the lived context, slowly maturing into a new sense of embodied awareness, with fading memories of past lives and former learning. A child may remember a past life, other parents, a difference circumstance, life events including a past death, but after a decade of new embodiment those memories can fade and even be denied, forgotten but not gone. (36:1)

The sentient principles of attraction and repulsion continue to exert influences on the choices we make, the people we encounter, and the relationships we form, some new, some old, and some repeatedly. The soul has a life beyond the temporal order of embodiment which is why embodied life can never be the fully measure of what it means to be human and self-aware. There are layers of both knowing and forgetting, soul carried impressions, *samskaras* from multiple past lives, subtle imprints. (36:2)

These imprints act subconsciously to influence behaviors or responses, seeds of past life deeds and outcomes, psychic tendencies lying quiescent until circumstances act to catalyze an impulse or desire. Through meditation we can gain insight into these impressions, in dreams we can observe their actions, and in relationships feel the tendency that at times unexpected, strange, or even alien. There is a disjunct between waking states and sleeping potential, a potential that is itself shaped by other lives. (36.3)

The challenge of integration does not simply refer to conscious states, but also to subconscious and hyperconscious tendencies that have been carried forward from other lived embodiments. The mind is by no means a "blank slate" (*tabula rasa*) but is in fact deeply conditional and shaped by past life, out-of-body encounters, and spiritual influences accessed through altered states, visions, and post-mortem transitions. The past is a living presence in the Now moment, what was still is, and what will be. (36:4)

Past life influences are carried through soul knowledge and often manifest in dreams, I have had many dreams of past lives, none historically known and most quiet lives seeking a better understanding of immediate lived experiences. But these experiences connect, they form themes, integral influences shaping choice and desire, usually as subconscious reactions not well comprehended by the waking mind. Waking up means recovering such impressions and recognizing subtle past life influences. (36:5)

Past life experiences can also shape collective tendencies; wars, famine, plagues, and other mass events leave their mark as well, creating a wide range of reactions carried unconsciously into another life and manifest in conditions similar to those past events. Collective fear can be a resubscription of past trauma, divided by diverse attitudes but shaping collective decisions and group affiliations, past negative shadows can fall across the new landscape, creating reactive culture patterns. (36:6)

At the other end of the spectrum, there is a transpersonal influence as well, where soul knowledge shines through the morass of subconscious tendencies bringing new patterns of illumination and deeper spiritual insights. The collective can be shaped by the positive influx of multiple spiritual realizations, by spiritual community members reborn into new circumstances but carrying the impressions of past spiritual life. The illumination of soul is not an end to rebirth but a new patterning, a new horizon. (36:7)

I remember my death in several lives, being met by an angelic being, guided into post-mortem domains, undergoing transformation, and then in astral flight finding a new birth through union with my new embodied parental birth-mother and father. Only a small portion of my soul was incarnate in pregnancy and only at the time of birth was my soul fully engaged but not yet fully embodied. As a newborn child soul, I was both in a new body and beyond that body, earthy and transpersonal, new and ancient. (36.8)

The transition to new life was a slow contraction, my expanded soul awareness slowly contracted to my body awareness, not as within the body but rather as surrounding the body with its own subtle soul-field. Body-in-soul is the correct image, not soul-in-body; and not a single field because the soul field was inseparable from the additional energetic fields of embodiment, the circulating neuropsychic, heart-pulse dynamics of flow throughout the entire structure of soul-embodied being. (36:9)

The conditionality of past experiences is as impactful as any past experiences, some act to reshape our awareness or we may bury the experience and not allow those past life impressions to move us from our habituated embodied paths of action. Our "past actions" (karma) do not have lineal causal effects, there is no necessary consequence to actions other than our circumstantial rebirth, our post-mortem choices, and complex principles of causality we do not actually comprehend or even recognize. (36:10)

Further past actions are collectively influenced, what we choose, how we act, is often shaped by collective circumstances, cultural expectations, personal relations, such that "will and choice" are often informed by social intentions. Free will is an abstraction, our will is more often shaped by conditionality, subconscious influences, memory, shared values, and our sense of group identity. Past life influences add to this complex mélange of causal consequences, a lineal theory of karma is much too limited. (36:11)

Our re-becoming is an act of nature, a sentient cycle of re-emergence that can lead to refinement, more subtle perceptions, and a much more extensive sense of the transhistorical continuum. When we wake up to past life influence, we discover the profound complexity of the matrix, our shared experiences informing how our relationships "meet and match" in a context of creative discovery and transformative spiritual awakening. Otherwise, we are sleepers, waking only partially to wonder. (36:12)

Highest Holy Realizations

Holy Mother, there is no highest realization,
only the peak and fullness of individual
insights, illuminations, enlightenments
leading to teachings, transitional
metaphors and spiritual memes
giving testimony to their
unique realizations,
abundant and
complex.

And yet, there is Realization, and
a height attained giving birth to
new vistas of perception and
comprehension, a holy view,
celebrating a visionary horizon
whose scope and depth may require
many generations of practitioners to
embrace and integrate, to truly comprehend.

How vast is this created cosmos!
How holy, sacred, luminous, and divine!

Holy Mother, Father of Light,
reveal the density and complexity of all
created life as a miracle of becoming,
not an accident but an intended
possibility whose form and
contents require individual
testimony gained through
direct encounter, a living
intensity of merging
held in the fragile

web of shared
illuminations.

The vessel of prayer, the boat of mediation,
the wings of illumined thought and the
glowing embers of an awakened heart,
a soulful longing for Thy Light, all
reflecting the intended gift of self
awakening, rising from the bed
of visionary dreams and then
transposed into actual
life patterns, imprints
whose impressions
last a multitude
of generations,
even more!

The Highest Holy Realizations
are all those that open a vista and then
share the insights as a gift given, not as
self-made constructs but as an imprint
on sand, knowing that the waves will
wash away all traces and absorb the
images and words into that Ocean
whose immeasurable depths
hold all realizations as a
precious treasure. We
give that gift that it
may be Returned
to its true
Maker.

Holy Mother guide our thoughts,
direct our aspirations, and teach us
the true paths to illumination!

May it be so!

The Gospel of Peace (37)

The "good news" (gospel) is that peace is a most worthy goal, one whose actualizations lead to even greater creativity, not in the name of any one teaching, but as integration of themes, each contributing to a shared global harmony. These themes reflect core values—compassion, kindness, sympathy, cooperation, moderation, justice, right relations, economic parity, respect, acknowledging difference—and many other such values that shape emergent collaborations, locally and transnationally. (37.1)

Each culture and community must shape its values accordingly, not through convergence, nor under threat of subordination, but through open choice motivated by a collective vision of the need for peace, life, and health over war, chaos, and death. It is an individual choice, a communal choice, a collective choice, grounded in sustained commitment to core values meant to sustain a greater maturity through non-violent cooperation at all levels of social and cultural organization. (37.2)

The primary responsibility falls upon the individual—to create peace, one must have higher value commitments leading to cooperation and a shared resolution of conflicts and disruptive challenges. A stable mind, a loving heart, a creative will, all contribute to this integration of values and associated actions. Good words, good thoughts, good deeds, good mind, good soul, good relations, can each foster positive outcomes without creating false narratives that would privilege one group (or individual) over another. (37.3)

Equal rights is a foundational principle of peace, only when justice is mediated in accord with higher value commitments can we expect a transformative outcome. The privileged mindset must be deconstructed in the light and wisdom of a spiritual realization that equality is not a matter of legal definition but a sacred testimony that values each and every living creature. This includes all species, it means the deprivileging of human superiority over all other species. Compassion requires equality. (37.4)

Equal rights includes animal rights, ecological rights, water rights, oceanic rights, making the task of a clean, pure, harmonious world part of the program of peaceful restoration of our global home. Om as the center of home represents peace in both the most local sense and in the most cosmic sense; Aum Shanti Aum, is the peace mantra, a rhythmic chant meant to provoke an inner realization. Peace is a core value whose realization requires inner work, a transformative, collective awakening. (37.5)

The gospel of peace is a sign, not an illusion nor fantasy, but a heart-centered expression of an inner soul desire to actually live and dwell in peace with others without oppression, greed, violence and anger shaping our cultural heritages. It is a sacred sign, a Christ-sign, where "anointed" means blessed by Spirit to live peacefully without censuring others, without blame or intolerance, without elevating our own faith or beliefs, to liberate ourselves from all apocalyptic narratives and condemnations. (37.6)

The gospel of peace is not a doctrine nor does it require allegiance to any one person or path; it is a non-exclusive set of values internalized as a foundation for enduring human, animal, world relations, combining love, wisdom, illumination, and true gnosis into the distillate of an integral realization emanating peace as actual Presence, as a gift whose luminous rays pervade a living cosmos of loving others. Peace is a state of mind, soul, and heart, not simply an ethic or value set. (37.7)

Peace is a co-creative work, a shared construct of many hearts and minds working together to strengthen our awareness of Being-With; we all participate in the process. Our individual attitudes and actions contribute to the weave or they can pick apart the threads and patterns. In my own life, I have embodied peace to the best of my ability, supporting the pattern in teaching spirituality—a comparative spirituality, a multi-sourced reservoir of possible healing paths, each offering the creation of a more mature world. (37.8)

The gospel of peace is not new but restructured in accord with values that do not prioritize one teaching but finds inspiration in all teachings. Many men and women have given eloquent testimony to paths of peace in multiple spiritual traditions, it is a worldwide ideal, the message is clear: choose cooperation and negotiation over threat and violence; choose equal justice for all, not for only one privileged group; choose humility and patience over dominance and discrimination. (37.9)

There is a profound Source at work, within, throughout, and beyond the immediate sensory world, a Presence that supports Being-With as a necessary ground for the formation of core values that support a healthy, peaceful world. Being-With means caring about your neighbors, distant others, and far-removed persons struggling to maintain a better way of life. It means standing is support of all those in need. (37.10)

It means cultivating a heart-centered way of life, one in which sympathy and compassion are guiding principles; it requires the recognition that we depend upon each other in support of an ideal that can only be realized through mutual efforts and enduring, shared commitments. Our Being-With is an indicator of the networks we form as a collective means to actualize that ideal, peace and diversity, stability and creative discovery, meaningful dialogue and personal realizations. (37.11)

The gospel of peace includes all creatures, all beings, high or low, every living creature part of our entire world, every subtle spirit, all entities in collaboration with the establishment of an uplifted world free from strife, poverty, and suffering. Every world is a jewel in the cosmic net and every harmonic world honors a gospel of peace as its most fundamental testimony of spiritual success. An uplifted world is one in which peace is a pervasive ethos that utterly encourages creative discovery, wisely developed. (37.12)

Christos-Sophia Unions (38)

The Hermetic pathway is best symbolized by the Holy Wedding of the Sophianic Bride with the Christos groom, and their multispectral children of all hues and colors. This is not one wedding but an innumerable festival of weddings in which there is both union and distinctness between each couple. This merging represents the comingling of genders, the infusion of multiple perspectives into a dynamic Whole shared by all such partners. This is a spiritual union that treasures each person, each talent, each love. (38.1)

The Christos-Sophia union is also an alchemical sign, an anagogic indicator of how gender perspectives must merge and not lose their individual character or emphasis while also blending and sharing core values and practices. Sophia (Eros) brings intuitive wisdom, spontaneity, emotional depth and overflowing grace to all beings; Christos (Logos) brings dedicated commitment, respectful insight, structure, analysis, and an articulate ethos of shared values and creative compassion. (38.2)

Together, each contributes to the fullness they represent as a binary pair open to a Third Presence—Eros plus Logos leading to Kallos, Beauty, a sacred bond of enduring vows. This marriage occurs in the heart of each seeker, between seekers who embody the principles of Hermetic gnosis. Each seeker cultivates the alchemical union of feminine-masculine integration, learning from living examples of every gender orientation. Genders multiply, create differences, Beauty cannot be contained in a single pair. (35.3)

Third Presence is a gift, a realization of enduring value, saturating the entire horizon of a long life lived in Spirit with kindness as a guiding ethos of principled action and thinking. This marriage endures, through all the trials, tribulations, and challenges of everyday life because it is rooted in Spirit-Beauty, enlivened by deep roots that reach into the Ever Now. This marriage reflects utmost commitment to each aspect, each partner, both Sophia and Christos, to wisdom and value-centered actions. (38.4)

The Sophia-Christos relation is like a circle within which a sacred rite is performed, an invocation of subtle Presence meant to guide an outcome or actualize a possibility. This ritual corresponds to cosmic principles, nature (Sophia) and cosmos (Christos) as partners in sustaining the World Soul, the Third Presence that endures. Step outside the sacred circle and secular life dominates, skepticism runs riot, and doubt and blame become allies in sowing confusion and loss of deeper purpose. (38.5)

This circle can encompass the entire world by blending with other circles, not by subsuming, but through cooperation, shared borders, overlapping concerns, and communal interests uniting highly diverse practitioners of multiple faiths and spiritual paths. The circle has permeable boundaries, into which sacred energies and subtle beings may enter, seeking to support the activities of the heart that motivate action and response in the circle. The response flows out of the circle and into the shared world. (38.6)

Our collective becoming depends on many diverse circles, tens of thousands, millions, as a testament of committed, responsible beings seeking to bring peace and wisdom to a turbulent world caught in the dynamics of spiritual evolution. Christos teaches love and healing, Sophia teaches insight and illumination, and Spirit teaches the enduring truths of an evolving cosmos open to the Infinite. In the Ever Now there are many paths and the Hermetic teaching is only one among a vast plurality. (38.7)

I have known marriage, separation, and remarriage, the breaking and healing of the heart, through love lost and found, as part of the Hermetic path; not all relationships endure, sometimes separation is necessary and the best path. It is not easy and the outcome remains hidden in the clouds of change and transformation. But Sophia endures, Christos exemplifies, and Spirit leads us toward those right relations that correspond to our dedicated search for mature integration and partnership. (38.8)

My second marriage endures, representing a warming flame in the midst of change and struggle, giving hope, comfort, and grounded love deep down. The third marriage, the inner union of Christos-Sophia also endures, heightens the horizon and deepens the core, expanding the present Now into a circle encompassing the far past and distant future. This sacred heart union reflects an actual path, embraced by many and differentiated according to insight, talent, and flexible, responsible ethics. (38.9)

Sophia-Christos is a luminous node, a jewel made of life-force energies, a syntropy of creative discovery, unveiling the hidden and unseen potentials of soulful-being. It manifests as the third-eye opening on the vast horizons of cosmic life where psychic exchange flows unbrokenly across an immense expanse, intertwined with worlds upon worlds, a psychocosm of indescribable beauty, luminosity, and intelligence. This union of heart-soul is not simply local and cultural, but cosmic and universal. (38.10)

Sophia-Christos images the heart with the holy Ankh, the Tau Ra, the mediating sign of the male-female union, a golden, looped cross with a centered ruby jewel, transforming into a brilliant diamond whose light dissolves all forms and whose subtle rays illumine the hidden energies of the world-cosmos. This light is full spectrum, all shades and colors, reaching far beyond the natural eye and opening a vista on the Infinite; every energy, subtle plasmic wave, gravitational eddy, reflects that Light. (38.11)

The Christo-Sophia harmonic is a musical composition that animates physical life with the energies of compassion and wisdom insights; it contains the disparate clank of center lost, atonal shards of confusion, and the swelling randomness of possibilities, layered with chaos. The boundaries are transparent but inner stability provides the enduring ground for discovery and creative expression, not classic, not traditional, but unique, an unfolding gestalt of harmonic love newly expressed, our mutual find. (38.12)

The Hermetic Testament (39)

This work is a testament, a narrative soliciting Spirit through the context of personal discovery and shared wisdom. It teaches endurance, dedication, and commitment to this world transformation; not escape or denial, but affirmation and full incarnation. The Hermetic view is one of world transformation, an uplift through Mystery and Being to a more luminous, shared participatory spirituality. This is a path of present, future, and past becoming, a timeless arc in the unending Ever Now. (39.1)

The source of the testament is Spirit engraved on the human heart as a sacred act of discovery; not on one heart, but on a multitude of hearts, minds, souls, all desiring true awakening to inner potential, uniquely realized. It is an individual path with many byways and alternatives, not a synthetic mélange, but a well-defined distinctiveness meant to inspire beyond the words themselves. What matters is both stability and discovery, cohesiveness and creative expression, maturity and spontaneity. (39.2)

The Hermetic Testament is a sign, an indicator of great changes that are occurring, the emergence of new spiritualities, new visions of future becoming, more voices joined in the articulation of world awakening. This shared vision has many forms, and possible pathways leading to illumination; the Hermetic Testament is one such pathway, a multipath, a journey or pilgrimage to honor Spirit and Mystery free of any coercive mentality. It is a path of peace, hope, and intelligent dedication. (39.3)

A Testament of peace recognizes the suffering of others as motivation for change leading to a world based in care, preservation, and support for all beings. Suffering is the consequence of indifference, false privileges, and corrosive, immoral behaviors; only when we wake up to our true responsibilities will we begin to understand the message of suffering. The message is clear, suffering will endure until we take full responsibility for the well-being and safety of others. Every person shares this responsibility. (39.4)

The Hermetic teaching points toward a realization, a spiritual awakening whose ground is the very Source of All-Becoming; we seek to embody the many virtues that best promote healing, love, intelligence, and spiritual maturity. The goal is a share spiritual awakening, not just personal enlightenment, but a collective realization creating a vast network of co-workers each contributing to global transformation. What is local is also global, what is global must also be local. (39.5)

In this process of awakening, gnosis plays a crucial role, not one realization but many types and kinds, a topology of spiritual differences, each contributing to a harmonic understanding of what is possible. The core values hold the center in creative flux and flow, love is not diminished and hope is a trustworthy star, creative intelligence guides, and moral actions preserve. We each embody the ideal, not one person but a community whose members respect their differences even while acting in concert. (39.6)

Diversity allows for difference and cooperation set the limits where differences would misalign; each can contribute and each can go his or her own way, the choice is simple—give what you can and pursue your spiritual goals in harmony with others. We do not need leaders or followers, what we need is partnership, purpose, and commitment to a way of life that exemplifies Spirit. Do you lead such a life? Do you exemplify your spiritual virtues as worthy of notice? Do you teach through your actions? (39.7)

I spent many years searching the archives of history for worthy teachings, from many traditions, eras, and countries. In the end I found good in every tradition and also limits and problems, no tradition lacks its imperfections and each offers valuable insights and guidance. I found the Hermetic Way most appealing due to its open horizons and alchemical languages, a visionary collection of diverse teachings. I saw a feminine aspect at its core, a mediation directed toward synthesis and gnosis. (39.8)

This gnosis is a living connection to Spirit, a vibrant sense of Presence whose touch is a soothing grace and whose teachings are multiple and complex. The Hermetic Testament is a temple witness to the teachings of the sages, including those whose time has yet to come, a light leading to luminous future realizations meant to affirm our capacity to cross-over into new wisdom and insight. There is a prophetic mandala inscribed in the heart of the Testament, yet to be revealed. (39.9)

There is also a promise, that at the heart of utmost striving and spiritual desire, there is a profound Truth, the reality of Spirit born of Spirit, through the matrix of soul, mind, and body. When these three unite, become integral to Spirit, luminous with Presence, then the flame is lit and the temple receives its fullness in grace and light. Only then will the true depths be seen and known, a vastness so great and a volume so expansive that no one vision can possibly express its full potential. (39.10)

The Hermetic Testament points toward the future, toward a time when war has no place, violence is subdued, and peace is a natural expression of cosmic harmonies. Such a time will require a divestment of attachments to needs no longer relevant to an era in which cooperation is a natural function of global relations. This will occur through individual awakening, positive collective efforts, and a just and fair assessment of all motives expressed in human interactions. Peace requires peaceful beings. (39.11)

There is no end to these teachings, the future remains open, many horizons yet unexplored, new discoveries, greater clarity of cosmic truths, and a much deeper realization of the sacred human, and others, potential. This is an arrow pointing toward a different path in which each finds the markers necessary for true illumination. Every person is a possible means for discovery and every discovery must be assessed collectively. We move forward together and individually; such is the path. (39.12)

No Final Transformation (40)

There is no final transformation because there is no predictable end nor any sense in which "enlightenment" is a final stage of all human development; all is in process and creatively there is much more to discover. The goal of enlightenment remains a legitimate and viable goal, a personal and transpersonal realization, a fully actualized condition of mergence and unity consciousness. But such a realization is only one possible outcome among a multitude of other possible creative becomings. (40.1)

The process of spiritual discovery, as a form of knowing, insight, and understanding is not limited to specific states of psychic realization; Spirit overflows and Being Becomes beyond the limits of any given species or teaching. This overflow is itself an opening of horizons that allows for new synthesis, transforming awareness into new types of perception and unveiling the multilayered metacosm. Enlightened states may well participate in and assimilate these emergent domains, holding open the vista for other realizations. (40.2)

However, there are transtemporal aspects to these realizations as they merge into the atemporal qualities of the Ever Now, attaining a perspective in which quantitative time or *chronos* is no longer a measure of process. Imagine the temporal order of events as a two-dimensional plane, past and future, while a third dimension supports a participant observer able to see "beyond time" through Ur-space, through the Metacosm. Such knowing has no end goal, only an endless opportunity to observe and learn. (40.3)

The Ever Now is not a temporal concept but a spiritual intuition of a *timeless present* in which all knowledge is syntropically available however far or distant its origins may be in past or future becoming. The Ever Now is Infinite and Evolving, all containing, always in process, never ceasing in overturning novelty into knowledge and time into an artifact of measure meant to create a finite base for embodied perceptions. The soul is an atemporal entity, both in time and beyond time, both subject to temporal process and Infinity. (40.4)

Soul perceptions can accommodate parapsychic intuitions based in past life, future becoming, and transtemporal awareness in the multilayered creativity of the Imaginal. We can imagine a multidimensional Metacosmos, precognitive, prophetic insights, retrocognitive readings of present objects carrying past impressions, out of body experiences exploring the multidimensions of the World Soul and the sentient energies and impression of other worlds and beings far beyond Terra Firma. (40.5)

There is no final transformation because we each participate in the unending processes of on-going psychic discovery in which all beings share varying degrees of participant awareness. In the full-spectrum sense, the Ever Now becomes a viable basis for understanding transtemporal perceptions, how emergence and discovery flow forth from a Super-Existent, primal Depth, timeless and unending. At the heart of this process is an intelligible, compassionate, caring nurture, a sacredness ever evolving. (40.6)

Not made in any human image or, if made in human image, then only transitional to a realization that the Infinite has infinite forms imaging a formless potential into viable shapes, an autopoiesis whose outcomes arise through the entirety, from a Wholeness that lacks no capacity for future creative expression. Why imagine a final goal, why cling to a fixed end? When in fact, endless creativity over-lights all becoming. (40.7)

I once believed in final ends, enlightenment, satori, self-realization, all held up as ideal ends, but limited to explicit forms of realization; then I woke up and realized that there was no final goal, that all spirituality was a form of becoming in the exploration of human (and other) potential. That all that was, is, and shall be cannot exhaust an Infinite potential whose full expression requires an entire universe for its realization and perhaps, endless recycles that further refines and overcomes past limits. (40.8)

Enlightenment is real, an actual creative occasion, a burst of light opening a horizon on the Infinite and filling the heart-mind-soul of the perceiver with grace and presence blessing him or her and their community. But such a realization is only one among many, each with its own unique character and emphasis, each distilling a portion of Whole into a view the reflects how the part and the whole merge into something greater than either. Something greater than the Whole? Yes, an uncontainable Overflow. (40.9)

The part cannot contain the whole and the whole is only a reference to something that has no boundaries or limits; the Whole references All That Is as a limitless indefinite, a horizon that disappears over the rim of the visible cosmos where space and time no longer hold sway and swimmers there merge and reemerge to find there is no end to their transformations. Imagine an unending process in which beings of all kinds, physical, psychic, or transphysical, cannot exhaust the possibilities of Becoming. (40.10)

There are plateaus and peaks, valleys and hidden caves, long stretches of similarity and sudden bursts of change and confrontation, all part of the process of discovery. Even enlightenment takes many decades to assimilate while there is yet a flow of other streams of knowing, a capacity for a shift of subtle insight, giving rise to a new understanding not part of "original experience"—such experience is only a stage in a much longer, more profound process of discovery. (40.11)

The stability of a given revelation, of an illumined heart-mind, arises from an inner calm, an eye in the storm of transformation, creating an island of peace whose radiance sends healing rays into that storm, a call to others to gather and coalesce. There are many such islands, many hidden, all dedicated to the healing and restoration of the many. And more islands yet to form, more illuminations whose rays will extend further the possibilities of becoming, such is the path of our shared transformations. (40:12).

Afterword

The passion is not spent, nor the light dimmed, but the flame passes as it must to others, to other lights, other teachings, new ideas, and old truths mixed. The spiral road must cycle through its repetitions, even while expanding, where points on each cycle form a direct line to the center. All the southern points reflect a nostalgia for times past when opportunities were less obvious but more abundant. All the northern point predict a forthcoming, a time of change, transformation, a shared awakening. The eastern and western points balance out, creating both inner reality and outer becoming, balanced insofar as the points matter and are not forgotten. The cycles are ladened with time, point by point, by the illusion that time is the key to measure progress. But time is not the true measure, only the rhythm, pace, step and beat of multiple progressions retarded by our clinging to what was with no sure sense of what must become.

We are each a point on the cycle, a living breathing being whose thoughts, desires, aspirations and actions shape an outcome, a resonance, vibrant when fully spiritualized and contracted when self-absorbed. We must open to the points of others, not remain self-enclosed enamored by only our own thoughts and ideals, must be able to abandon our grasp on what has become in order to dwell fully in the Now. We give birth and then having done our best to raise a child, we give him or her freedom to discover what may or may not become. Love says fly free and also, do not forget your origin, nor your parents, nor your ancestral lineage which gives you ground and soul in greater abundance than self alone. The message is given, the gnosis is communicated, the insight is established, the lasting effect is yet to be fully learned. Beyond the timeless wave, there is knowledge and within the wave it appears in stages, every stage and opportunity, every misstep, another opportunity.

Having given what is possible on the fringe of the impossible, I close with a single thought, perhaps, after the timeless wave, there will be more thoughts shared in concert with what written here. The goal is to create metalogical connections, associations and emergent patterns of shared insight. This is the opening of a dialogue, discussion, discernment meant to foster communication across multiple branes, intersections within the known extended into the emergent. The unknown is discoverable, through multiple perspectives whose authors share a vision which is itself developmental and on-going. There is no closure in texts, no terminus in the written word, each syllable is a sound meant to suggest, a rhythm, a song or poem offered to facilitate appreciation. Here is a threshold where critical thought meets its own limitations, based on a deeper intuition that what is truly critical requires letting-go and dropping pretensions. Judgment is less important than appreciation if the effort merits genuine regard.

Truth is a fragile creation, often nothing more than social convention supported by an ethos of authority meant to sustain a shared point of view. All such truth is relative, just as the truths of this writing are relative, nothing stands eternal in material form. All texts mush pass, all words collapse over time into the truisms of forgotten origins. And yet, some texts endure because they are found meaningful even long after their creation. A relative truth does not mean necessarily transient, rather it means enduring insights whose relative value is dependent upon the emphasis and use to which those insights are applied. Take what seems important, relevant, worth remembering, let everything else remain in the flow of possible new insights in the future. We stand together on a vast horizon of discovery, where some words are more valuable than others, while other words remain hidden in the folds of our immediate prehensions.

Tomorrow never comes, it is aways today, the Now moment, and in that moment past and future vanish into that far-reaching horizon where all words resonate creating a vast network of possible meanings not yet fully comprehended. But even when comprehended, those same words lead to other associations whose tacit meanings overflow beyond the constraints of specific thoughts and ideas. Far beyond those ideas are other forms, entities, spaces and branes unknown and yet resident within the shared horizon. This horizon cannot be exhausted and no amount of words will ever reveal its full contents. There is a poetry, a spiritual song, whose tempo, assonance, and metaphors reflect a hint of that greater reality. We open our hearts to those songs and realize there are many, many singers, far more than what we know or even begin to recognize. That is why standing on the edge requires utmost humility, without that luminous virtue we are deaf and blind to what really occurs. To truly see and hear, we must confirm the limitations of our own understanding in order to surpass the limits which bind us to lesser truths. The perception of truth is an expression of soul life, and soul is the medium by which we comprehend all that is truly beyond our present comprehensions. May creative peace be our ever-lasting goal! Selah! Salaam! Light and Love!

Lee Irwin / Sirr al-Basir
Island Earth

APPENDIX ONE

Holy Mother Spirit Vision

This event occurred while I was wide awake, during the day while I was active and busy with everyday tasks of teaching. My mind was very concentrated but also very quiet in a deep sense. There was a trigger, which I cannot remember, something subtle that initiated an insightful thought that impacted me with great force. Perhaps it was after talking with someone about the importance of the divine feminine while walking back to my office. Suddenly, the thought struck me deeply, not consciously constructed, but a sudden swelling forth, "I am an apostle of the Holy Mother Spirit." I felt a deep impact in my body, there was a truthfulness to this thought that I was not expecting, a psychic arousal that compelled me to think about these words. What could it mean?

As I deliberated on this thought-word impression, I realized that it was a powerful elemental intuition, one with great potential for good. I looked up the phrase "Holy Mother Spirit" and was pleased to find that Mother Teresa, the great Catholic Saint of India, had used the phrase. It was a phrase resonant with Holy Spiritual presence, a calling that could be embraced, a teaching that could be articulated. My next inspirational thought was, "There is nothing excluded in the Holy Mother Spirit — all paths are given life by that Presence." This insight compelled me to regard the Holy Mother Spirit, the Holy Mother Light, as the incarnational ground of Presence, the active Shakti of all created life, all living beings, all forms, and energies, all spirit beings great and small. There was an underground church, the Church of the Living Presence, the holy spiritual that was imbued with feminine nurture that supported all aspects of spiritual being. There are others who use this phrase of Holy Mother Spiritual before I, creative others, men and women, I'm receiving it, holding it, nurturing it.

What did "apostle" mean? I looked it up — apostle in Greek means "an ambassador, one set apart, one with a message, one sent out" ("with signs and wonders, and mighty works" 2 Cor 12:12; Jesus as apostle Heb 3:1). But an apostle of what? — of the Holy Mother Spirit, not Christ, not God, but specifically a Holy Spiritual calling to carry a message of the Holy Spirit Mother, Spirit, Spirit Holy, Holy Spirit Mother, Spirit Light, Holy Mother Spirit.

But then, another visionary stage unfolded having greater symbolic form and content. I held my distance from the energies of this up-swelling presence, at the same time, reflecting on its form in terms of a sign or symbol. Again and again, the Ankh kept coming to me — "this is the sign of the Holy Mother Spirit, neither male nor female, but both and neither." I could see it in my body, in my heart, a silver Ankh with a lustrous pearl, a moonstone, a fire opal at its intersection. I could see in my third eye, over my head, below my feet, inverted at the base of my spine and an energy flowing between this and the one upright over my head. Then the silver Ankh transformed into a golden Ankh with a bright red ruby at its intersection, like a drop of blood, the blood on the white spear of the Grail. And then this golden Ankh held a diamond gem, refracting multicolored lights, a full spectrum of energies below and above the human norm.

I could see the Holy Mother Spirit in my heart as a beautiful white lotus with green leaves with an aura of golden light and over it, floating, the golden Ankh and the blood ruby in the center was a sign of feminine blood in monthly flow as life force and procreative power and it was also male blood given in sacrifice for the healing of others. When the blood runs down the Ankh, it drops slowly, drop by drop, onto the open heart of the lotus where it is absorbed infinitely, thus energizing the life force of the increasing magnitude of the flower's brilliance and as it grows brighter, the flow of blood ceases, and there is pregnancy, and the ruby is transformed into a diamond light, illumining rays breaking forth, absorbing the flower, the image, the energy, and becoming a Holy Mother Spiritual, a presence concealing the inner form of the flower (November 2004).